26 Italian Songs and Arias

AN AUTHORITATIVE EDITION BASED ON AUTHENTIC SOURCES

John Glenn Paton, editor

A high quality recording of all of the piano accompaniments, recorded by Joan Thompson, is available on cassette tape and compact disc from your favorite music dealer or directly from the publisher. See back cover for prices. When ordering from the publisher, please send a check adding $2.00 for postage and handling.

Table of Contents

Preface

In this collection are some of the world's most famous arias. Everywhere, serious students of classical singing learn these arias, and famous artists perform them in recitals. Do we really need a new edition of them? Yes, because we still have not heard them as their composers meant for them to sound.

Most of the arias in this collection were written in the 1600s and 1700s by composers who were intent on expressing their feelings and entertaining their listeners. They were not much interested in the past and they did not imagine that musicians of the future would care about them. They expected to be present whenever their music was rehearsed and performed, and so they wrote down a bare minimum of instructions for the performers.

In the 1800s, influenced by Romanticism, people began to look to the past as well as to the future in the arts. Musicians organized concerts of "ancient music," music that sometimes was only a century old. For the first time there was a market for the publication of music from previous centuries, and collections of older Italian arias were printed, especially in Paris, London, and Milan.

Motivated by both idealism and profit, some musical editors of the 1800s believed that they could make "ancient music" more appealing by making radical changes in the music. For instance, they:
- altered harmonies that seemed rough or dissonant to them.
- eliminated long vocal runs, which were out of fashion in the late 1800s.
- altered rhythms to make them less dance-like.
- added tempo markings that are too slow, and expression marks that overly romanticize the style.
- added accompaniments in a late Romantic pianistic style.

Some musicians of the 1800s believed that they were justified in "modernizing" the music of the 1600s and 1700s. This approach reached an extreme in the publications of Pietro Floridia, who preserved only the melodies of the old arias. He discarded the original harmonies altogether, describing them as "obsolete, thin, uncertain... with all the limitations imposed by the imperfect scientific knowledge of those old times" (*Early Italian Songs and Arias*, Philadelphia: Oliver Ditson, 1924). Deprived of their authentic harmonies, Floridia's arrangements of Baroque arias sound like mediocre compositions of the 1920s.

We hold a different view now: the best composers of earlier times still have something important to give us. We can learn from them and enjoy their music if we have it in the most honest form possible.

If you have known these arias in other editions, you will find surprises in this one. Many errors have been corrected. Wrong notes, wrong words, and wrong composers' names have been set right wherever possible.

Most of the arias have been completely revised, using the earliest sources of information that could be found. If no early manuscript or printed source is known, the familiar version is left intact, with acknowledgment of the editor and date of publication.

On the page preceding each aria, the singer will find information that is vital to an expressive and stylistic performance of that aria. The Italian poem is printed in boldface. Above each Italian word, the pronunciation is shown by means of the International Phonetic Alphabet. Under each individual word is a literal translation into English. (Because of grammatical differences between English and Italian, the literal translations often are unclear; idiomatic translations are provided on the music pages for clarity.)

Dr. Arthur Schoep of the University of North Texas and Daniel Harris supplied the literal English translations. Square brackets, [ ], indicate that an Italian word is not necessary and should not be translated into English. Parentheses, ( ), are used for a word that is not present in Italian but is needed to make sense in English. A hyphen is used where the meaning of one Italian word requires more than one English word: for instance, "M'ami?" means "Do-you-love-me?"

The "Poetic Idea," as summarized by the editor, is intentionally terse—it is provided merely as a safeguard against misunderstandings. If the aria comes from an opera, that fact is mentioned here.

"Background" is the factual story that lies behind the song: this paragraph tells who wrote the aria, where, and for what kind of audience. A good music dictionary can supply more general biographical information and add to your sense of the composer's individual place in the world of music.

"Source" means what materials were used to prepare this edition and how it differs from the editions that have been available until now.

The music pages include two further translations of each poem: James P. Dunn's singable translations match the musical rhythms perfectly; and Dr. Schoep's idiomatic translations convey the meanings accurately in correct English word order. The idiomatic translations may be used as program notes for a recital.

For each aria, the vocal line is presented in the most authentic form available. The same is true of the bass line, or continuo, which in most cases is the only accompaniment the composer provided.

The primary sources of these arias seldom contain specific tempo, dynamic, or style markings. Those added by the editor are printed in gray to emphasize that they are only suggestions.

The arias in this book are arranged in the historical order of their composers, so that by hearing them in sequence one gets a feeling for the history of Italian music in the Baroque (1600- 1750) and Classical (1750-1830) periods. Now and then you may want to look at a map of Italy and pictures of the cities where famous composers lived so that you have a sense of them as real people who loved singing and music just as you do.

This book begins with a song from *Le nuove musiche* ("The New Music"), which was published to call attention to musical experiments that had been going on in Florence. "The new music" contrasted radically with the music of the preceding period, the Renaissance.

Renaissance vocal music was either sung in churches, where the Latin texts were not understood by most people, or in homes, where sociable people sang for their own enjoyment. In either case, singers did not sing with individualized, dramatic expression because they took on subordinate roles in groups.

Solo singing as we know it began when Giulio Caccini and others composed music so that a soloist sang dramatically, accompanied by instruments playing chords in the background. It became possible to sing whole plays on stage—the first operas. This experiment was the basis of the new Baroque style.

An essential part of the new

style was the practice of writing bass-notes so that they indicated what chords should be played by the accompanying instruments. A typical small performing ensemble was a singer, a cello, and a harpsichord or lute. The instruments played from a single line of music, called a *basso continuo* because it is always present. The cello sustained the bass-notes, which often had melodic interest that formed a counterpoint to the voice. The harpsichord added appropriate chords. How the chords were added was up to the player. Since few modern pianists know how to play from a basso continuo, modern editions must provide written-out piano parts.

The gradual transition to Classical style took place in the mid-1700s as composers wrote out accompaniments more completely and composed more often for a full orchestra of strings and sometimes wind instruments. The subject matter of operas changed, as servants and working people became operatic characters (think of Rossini's *The Barber of Seville* and Mozart's *The Marriage of Figaro*).

Vocal styles did not change greatly; great singers were still international stars, and singers were still expected to master the art of vocal ornamentation. An excellent source of information is an exercise book that appeared at the end of the Classical period, Vaccai's *Practical Method of Italian Singing*, edited by John Glenn Paton (New York: G. Schirmer, 1974). The ornaments that Vaccai illustrated are valid for all composers in the Italian tradition throughout the Classical era.

In the Romantic era, composers exerted more control over performers and refused to allow singers to alter or ornament their music. As music was written out in more and more detail, it became customary to sing only the notes that were written. On the other hand, performers were expected to "interpret" the music with frequent variations in dynamics and tempo. In a highly Romantic style of performance, every phrase may contain some crescendo or diminuendo, accelerando or ritardando. The paradoxical result is that in Romantic style, the performer is true to the notes of the piece, but gives them a personal twist.

This view of Romantic performance style explains why editors who published older music were inclined to add expression markings that altered the character of the music. Some such markings are helpful, but others convey a false impression of the music.

Another paradoxical product of Romanticism is the phenomenon of artistic forgeries: a reverence for the past led to a desire to create works that matched the Romantic image of the past. The last two songs in this collection are such forgeries, and it is appropriate to perform them in Romantic style.

Good Style in Italian Singing

Baroque and Classical composers gave few instructions about musical performance; they did not foresee that future musicians would be interested. Even tempo, dynamics and style are usually left to our imaginations. We have great freedom, therefore, and great responsibility when we perform early music.

Keep in mind that expression of the words was Caccini's first priority and the motivation behind the Baroque movement. Even if your listeners do not understand Italian, they expect you to know what the words mean and to sing every word clearly. Know what each single word means, and then put yourself into the frame of mind of the character whom you are portraying. Practice speaking the words aloud with a clear, well-supported voice before you sing them. Vowels in Italian are much more important than consonants; only double consonants and rolled r's are emphasized.

Beautiful tone is expected at all times, and later Baroque composers wrote long legato runs to display singers' beautiful voices. Naturally, accurate intonation and consistent vocal quality depend on developing a secure breath technique.

While it is inherently dramatic, the Italian singing that we are studying is also a courtly art, one of graciousness and good manners. The texts are invariably about aspects of love, including joy, doubt, jealousy, and a thousand other variations, but never extending to vulgarity or violence.

The singer always appeals to the sympathy of genteel listeners, who will be offended if the singer is too self-indulgent. Erratic tempos, extreme ritardandos, facial grimaces, and uncontrolled gesticulation may be regarded as musical bad manners. Dynamic extremes, loud or soft, are hardly ever desirable.

When choosing a tempo, consider how many songs even today are written in dance-rhythms. For instance, several arias in this book are minuets, and they sound well when performed with an even, danceable tempo. Metronomes were invented around 1800, so metronome markings in early music are merely editors' opinions.

Throughout the Baroque and Classical eras, singers were considered the most important musicians; they were better paid than composers and more in demand in foreign countries. Singers were also highly trained musicians, who could read and learn music quickly and add ornaments tastefully. The best singers could improvise ornaments, so that no two performances were identical.

This edition includes suggestions for melodic ornamentation printed in cue-sized notes, but these are models only. Feel free to sing ornaments or not, as you prefer. After gaining some experience with this style, you may prefer to invent your own ornaments.

The best ornaments do three things at once:
- they make the music more expressive; for instance, a trill might symbolize a tremor of excitement in the voice;
- they clarify the music; for instance, by calling the listener's attention to an important cadence;
- they display the singer's voice; for instance, by demonstrating flexibility and wide range.

An important rule: an ornament must always sound as if it is easy for you. If it sounds uncertain or laborious, leave it out. For this reason alone, it is important to know which notes are original and which are ornaments, and this edition always makes that distinction clear.

A final word about pitch: if the range of a song is uncomfortable for you, feel free to transpose it to a higher or lower key. Music was often transposed in the 1600s and 1700s. Pitches were lower before 1800 than they are today. For instance, Scarlatti's C was almost the same as the pitch we call B today. It is always more important to make beautiful tones than to sing some specific high or low pitch.

Good Style in Accompanying

Much of what has been said about vocal style applies to Baroque and Classical instrumental music, which is also both dramatic and courtly. It is of basic importance that the pianist, as well as the singer, must understand what the text of the song says. In addition, certain technical things need to be said, especially to pianists who have not played much early music.

Most of the keyboard accompaniments given here are realizations of figured or unfigured bass parts. They approximate the style in which experienced players improvised. Other accompaniments are reductions of orchestral versions. In either case the performer should feel free to alter the accompaniments to suit the needs of the singer and the quality of the piano or other instrument played.

Rolled chords have been suggested, especially in songs that might have been accompanied by a lute or guitar. You may choose to break other chords in slow tempos, to add notes or re-voice chords, and to ornament the keyboard part to your liking.

Practically all early instruments made sounds that were softer and lighter than those of modern pianos. Even an accompaniment played by a full string orchestra was probably softer than the same notes played on a modern grand piano. Furthermore, any music composed before about 1770 was intended for a harpsichord, which has no sustaining pedal.

This music will sound best if it is played clearly and lightly.

Throughout this book, the lowest note of every chord is the bass note written by the composer. The bass part was played by a cello or a string bass or both, and a string bass sounds an octave lower than the written notes. Therefore it is often possible to double the bass notes an octave lower than written if you think that will give better support to the singer, considering the characteristics of the piano and the room where you are performing.

Many songs begin without any instrumental introduction. You can easily give the singer the correct pitch by playing a tonic arpeggio that ends on the singer's starting tone.

Sources of Accompaniments

Most of the aria accompaniments, whether they are continuo realizations or orchestral reductions, were made by the undersigned general editor on the basis of the earliest available sources, either manuscript or printed. Nos. 8 and 11 (in part) were contributed by Dr. Schoep, who also provided ornamentations for many of the arias. Gevaert's accompaniment for No. 12 has been kept as one of the better examples of editorial work in the 1800s. Nos. 5, 17 (perhaps spurious), and 20 are not trustworthy editions, but no authentic sources are available; attempted improvements could only be based on guesswork. Nos. 25 and 26 are published as written by their pseudonymous authors.

Acknowledgments

Thanks are expressed to the libraries mentioned in the source notes and to many others in the U. S. and abroad, to the helpful staff members of the libraries, and to the governments that support them. Much of the research was supported by a grant from the University of Colorado. That this research is now incorporated in a book is owing to the vision and integrity of Morton Manus, President of Alfred Publishing Co., who understood that even a best-seller should be altered if the alterations will make it more useful to musicians. Among the unfailingly helpful professionals at Alfred, Linda Lusk has had special responsibility for the innumerable details involved in musical editing. And always my love and thanks go to my wife, Joan Thompson, who has supported this work in every way.

John Glenn Paton
Los Angeles

"Amarilli, mia bella"

from *Le nuove musiche*
le nwɔve muzike

Giulio Caccini
dʒuljo kat:ʃini

Poetic idea

"You are my beloved, and you must believe that I am faithful to you." Despite the long tones and minor mode, this song is not sad, but rather persuasive and reassuring.

Background

Caccini was a tenor singer employed by the Medici family, who were the Dukes of Tuscany and famous patrons of art. Caccini was renowned for his singing and he accompanied himself on the archlute. His wife and children were also professional singers, and his daughter Francesca was a respected composer.

Source

(1) *Le nuove musiche*, Florence, 1601, re-published by Performers' Fac-similes, New York. For treble voice (G-clef) and continuo. Key: G minor, with a signature of one flat. Meter: four half-notes (four beats) per measure. For ease of reading, I have added bar-lines so that there are two half-notes (two beats) per measure.

Caccini called *"Amarilli"* a *madrigale*, a through-composed piece with uneven phrase-lengths; he used *aria* to describe strophic songs composed in dance rhythms.

In a few places the placement of syllables is changed to make shorter phrases. In m18 and m35 Caccini tied the first two notes and combined *to e* on the third note. In m25 and m42 Caccini wrote a dotted half-note, with *-li è il* slurred together on the dotted eighth. Caccini slurred m45 to the first note in m46 and combined *-li .è il* on the second note. Italian singers frequently adjust notes in these ways for the sake of comfort in breathing.

The familiar version of *"Amarilli"*, as edited by Alessandro Parisotti in *Arie Antiche*, vol. 1 (Milan: Ricordi, 1885), changes Caccini's music in still more ways. The incorrect meter signature of 4/4 causes singers to take the music too slowly, and the steady quarter-note movement makes the tempo too strict. The text *Prendi questo mio strale* ("Take my arrow") was changed to a gentler, less graphic line, *Dubitar non ti vale* ("To doubt does not avail you").

amaril:li mia bel:la
Amarilli, mia bella,
Amaryllis, my beautiful-one,

non kredio del mio kɔr doltʃe dezio
Non credi, o del mio cor dolce desio,
not do-you-believe, o of-[the] my heart sweet desire,

des:ser tu lamor mio
D'esser tu l'amor mio?
of-to-be you [the]-love my?

kredilo pur e se timor tas:sale
Credilo pur, e se timor t'assale,
Believe-it nevertheless, and if fear you-assails,

prendi kwesto mio strale
Prendi questo mio strale,
take this my arrow,

aprimil pet:to e vedrai skrit:toil kɔre
Aprimi il petto e vedrai scritto il core:
Open-to-me the bosom, and you-will-see written the heart:

amaril:li ɛil mioamore
Amarilli è il mio amore.
Amaryllis is [the] my love.

Amarilli, mia bella

Amarilli, my dear one

Guarini
English version by
James P. Dunn

Giulio Caccini (ca.1545-1618)
Edited by John Glenn Paton

Moderato, ♩ = 54 - 63

A - ma - ril - li, mia bɛl - la, Non
A - ma - ril - li, my dear one, Doubt

cre - di, o del mio cor dol - ce de - si -
not my lov - ing heart, you most a -

o, D'ɛs - ser tu l'a-mor mi - o?
dored, You a - lone my be - lov - ed.

Idiomatic translation: Amaryllis, my beautiful one, do you not believe, O my heart's sweet desire, that you are my beloved?

Believe it, nevertheless, and if fear assails you, take this arrow, open my bosom, and you will see written on my heart, "Amaryllis is my love."

Amarilli, mia bella

A page from *Le nuove musiche* by Giulio Caccini, published in 1601. The staff lines are not perfectly straight because they are made of many pieces of movable type, one for each musical symbol. Only the voice and continuo parts are given, along with a few numbers that indicate what chords the accompanist should play. Notice that the bass line has the F clef on the third line rather than on the fourth line; the first bass note is G. As a help for sight-reading, there is a mark at the end of each staff, which indicates the line or space of the first note on the next line.

"Lasciatemi morire!"

from *Arianna*
ari̯an:na

Claudio Monteverdi
kla̯udjo monteve̯rdi

Poetic idea

"I cannot live without my beloved. Nothing you do can comfort me." The person who sings this is Ariadne (or Arianna in Italian), the daughter of King Minos of Crete. Ariadne helped a foreign hostage, Theseus, to escape from death in the Labyrinth. Theseus took Ariadne to the island of Naxos, where he deserted her. Her grief is expressed in a long scene, which begins with the brief section given here. (In the end, Ariadne did not die. The god Dionysus married her and took her to live with the gods.)

Background

As a young composer Monteverdi published fine choral works in Renaissance style, but he adopted the new Baroque style wholeheartedly. As an employee of the Duke of Mantua, he certainly knew about the first opera performances and may have gone to hear them. When the Duke wanted an opera, he obtained a libretto, or opera text from Rinuccini, who had written the texts of the Florentine operas. Monteverdi wrote *Orfeo* in 1607 and *Arianna* the next year. The whole opera was a huge success; an eyewitness said that Arianna's lament "moved the ladies to tears." The lament became famous; it was sung all over Italy. The rest of the opera is lost.

Monteverdi's genius appears clearly in the first measure, in the wrenching dissonance between the voice and the bass part; nothing like it had ever been heard before.

Source

Manuscript Mus. G239, Biblioteca Estense, Modena, Italy. Another manuscript, in the handwriting of composer Luigi Rossi, British Library Add. 30491, is reproduced in *New

laʃ:ʃatemi mori̯re
Lasciatemi morire!
Let-me   die!

e   ke   vole̯te vo̯i ke mi konfɔ̯rte
E   che   volete   voi che mi conforte
And what do-wish you that me should-comfort

in kosi̯ du̯ra sɔ̯rte
In così dura sorte,
in such hard fate,

in kosi̯ gran marti̯re
In così gran martire?
in such great martyrdom?

Grove's Dictionary of Music and Musicians. For voice (soprano clef, starting on a1) and continuo. Original key: D minor, no signature. Meter signature: C, with irregular bar-lines. Bibliography: "Monteverdi's *Lamento d'Arianna*" by J. A. Westrup, *Music Review*, Vol. I, 1940.

The familiar version of "Lasciatemi morire!" edited by Parisotti in *Arie Antiche,* Vol. 2 (Milan: Ricordi, 1890), softened Monteverdi's music to suit the sentimental taste of the times. Parisotti altered the bass part to avoid the dramatic dissonances in m1 and m15, altered word accentuation in m11, and avoided other harsh and colorful harmonies. The harmonization in this edition is based on Monteverdi's madrigal version for five voices (1614).

Lasciatemi morire!

O soul, I long to perish!

Ottavio Rinuccini
English version by
James P. Dunn

Claudio Monteverdi (1567-1643)
Edited by John Glenn Paton
Vocal Ornamentation by Arthur Schoep

Lento, ♩ = 66 - 76

La - scia - - te - mi mo - ri - - re!
O soul, I long to per - ish!

La - scia - te - mi mo - ri - - re!
No more to live in an - guish!

E che vo - le - te voi che mi con - for - te
Think you to com - fort me, or give me sol - ace,

Idiomatic translation: Let me die! And what consolation is there for me,

enduring such a cruel fate, in such suffering? Let me die!

Lamento d'Arianna del Signor Claudio Monteuerde.

Afciatemi mo rire lafciate-

mi morire e chi volete voi che mi conforte

in cofi dura forte in cofi gran martire la-

fciatemi morire la fciate mi morire.

Lasciatemi morire!

In Monteverdi's opera *Arianna* (1608) this aria was accompanied by string instruments. This version, printed in 1623 in Venice, has only the voice and continuo parts.

"Monteuerde" is one of the accepted spellings of his name. The voice part is in soprano clef; the lowest line is middle C. Some accidentals in the bass line are not placed directly before notes; they are present to indicate whether the thirds of certain chords are major or minor.

Many details suggest that Monteverdi did not proofread this publication. The highly expressive chromatic ascent of the second phrase, present in all other sources, is missing from this one, and there are wrong notes elsewhere.

"Vittoria, mio core!"

Giacomo Carissimi

dʒakomo karis:simi

Poetic idea

"How happy I am! Love is over and I am free again!"

Background

Carissimi was a singer and organist who made his career in Rome as a church musician and later a Jesuit priest. A great choral composer, he was also known for his solo cantatas, which were sung by professional singers who entertained in the homes of the wealthy. *"Vittoria"* is one of about 150 cantatas by Carissimi, most of which are much longer and more complex.

Performance

Some early copies of *"Vittoria"* use the word *"vil"* as in m14, but others omit it and slur the first syllable of *"servitù"* as in m32. You may choose either version.

Some manuscripts have only one stanza, which results in the form ABA, and others have two, resulting in the form ABABA. If you prefer to sing only one stanza, then go directly from m53 to m74. If you wish to sing two stanzas, return from m53 to m2, then skip from m33 to m54 and finish the song. Either way is satisfactory.

Source

Manuscript Mus. G 28 at Biblioteca Estense, Modena. A facsimile of another manuscript is in *The Italian Cantata*, vol. 2 (New York: Garland, 1986). *"Vittoria"* exists in at least thirteen early manuscripts, which indicates its popularity. It was published in Rotterdam in 1656, but may have been composed as early as the 1630s. For voice (soprano clef) and continuo. Original key: D major, no signature (a ms. in Rome is in C). Meter: 3.

The familiar version was published by F. A. Gevaert in *Les Gloires de L'Italie* (Paris: private subscrip-tion, 1868). Gevaert worked from a Paris manuscript which has wrong notes in m5, resulting in an unre-solved dissonance with the bass.

REFRAIN

vit:tɔrja mio kɔre
Vittoria, mio core!
Victory,   my   heart!

non lagrimar pju
Non lagrimar più!
Not weep   longer!

ɛ ʃɔlta damore
È sciolta d'amore
Is free   of-love

la vil servitu
La vil servitù.
the abject slavery.   end refrain

FIRST STANZA:

dʒa   lempja   twɔi dan:ni
Già   l'empia   a' tuoi danni,
Formerly the-inhuman (one) to your sufferings,

fra   stwɔlo di zgwardi
Fra   stuolo   di sguardi,
among quantity of glances,

kon vet:si budʒardi
Con vezzi   bugiardi
with charms false

dispoze ʎ:ʎingan:ni
Dispose gl'inganni.
arranged the-deceits.

le frɔdi, ʎ:ʎaf:fanni
Le frodi, gl'affanni,
The frauds, the-pains

non an:no pju lɔko
Non hanno più loco.
not have   more place.

del krudo suo fɔko
Del crudo suo foco
Of-the cruel her fire

ɛ spɛnto lardore
È spento l'ardore.
is spent   the-ardor.

SECOND STANZA:

da   lutʃi ridɛnti
Da   luci ridenti
From lights smiling

non ɛʃ:ʃe pju strale
Non esce più strale
not dart more arrow,

ke   pjaga mortale
Che   piaga mortale
that (a) wound mortal

nel pɛt:to mav:venti
Nel petto   m'avventi.
in-the chest to-me-hurls.

nel dwɔl nɛ tormɛnti
Nel duol, ne' tormenti
In[-the] sadness, in[-the] torments

io pju non mi   sfat:ʃo
Io più non mi   sfaccio.
I more not myself undo.

ɛ rɔt:toɲ:ɲi lat:ʃo
È rotto ogni   laccio,
Is broken every snare,

sparito il timore
Sparito il timore.
gone-away the fear.

Vittoria, mio core!

Victorious, my heart is victorious!

Domenico Benigni
English version by
James P. Dunn

Giacomo Carissimi (1605-1674)
Vocal ornamentation by Arthur Schoep
Accompaniment realized by John Glenn Paton

Idiomatic translation: Victory, my heart! Do not weep any more. The abject slavery of love is dissolved.

(First stanza) Formerly the evil one, to make you suffer,

Note: For the shorter version of the aria, skip from m53 directly to m74 ("Vit-toria!"). For the longer version, return to m2, sing through m33, then follow the coda sign to m54 ("Da luci").

with many glances, with false charms set her traps. The fraud, the pain no longer take place.
The ardor of her cruel fire is extinguished. (Second stanza) From her smiling eyes no

longer darts and arrow that hurls a mortal wound into my chest.
In sadness, in torment I no longer tear myself to pieces. Every snare is broken; fear has disappeared.

"Che fiero costume"

Giovanni Legrenzi
dʒovaːni legrɛntsi

Poetic idea

"I am amazed at the power of love, whom others have described as just a blind baby boy!"

Background

Legrenzi played the organ at major churches in northern Italy and also composed 19 operas. Like Monteverdi before him, he directed the music at St Mark's Cathedral in Venice at the end of his life.

While many cantatas were composed primarily for professional singers to sing in private concerts, Legrenzi's cantatas were published and therefore were available to a wider public. This is typical of Venice, which was a republic and had a more democratic character than the other Italian states.

Source

Cantata found in *Echi di riverenza*, Op. 14 (Bologna: 1678). The other movements are a recitative and an aria. Photo-reproduction in *The Italian Cantata*, vol. 6 (NY: Garland, 1986). For voice (soprano clef, starting on a1) and continuo. Original key: A minor. Meter: 12/8.

In 1680 Legrenzi re-used this melody in his opera, *Eteocle e Polinice*, with the words *"Festeggia mio core"* ("Celebrate, my heart"). Curiously, it was not sung in the 1675 premiere of the opera nor in later productions. In the opera a string orchestra introduced the aria and occasionally echoed the singer.

The familiar version of *"Che fiero costume"* was edited by Carl Banck in *Arien und Gesänge älterer Tonmeister* (Leipzig: Kistner, 1880). Banck shifted the barlines to make the rhythm heavier and more dramatic and gave the aria an elaborately pianistic accompaniment in the late Romantic style.

ke fjɛro kostume
Che fiero costume
What (a) fierce custom

dalidʒero nume
D'aligero nume,
of-(a-)winged god,

kea fɔrtsa di pene si fatːʃadorar
Che a forza di pene si faccia adorar!
who by force of punishments himself should-make adored!

epːpur nelːlardore
E pur nell'ardore
And nevertheless in[-the-](my-)ardor

il dio traditore
Il dio traditore
the god traitorous

un vago sembjante mi feidolatrar
Un vago sembiante mi fe' idolatrar.
a lovely face me made to-worship.

ke krudo destino
Che crudo destino,
What (a) cruel fate,

keun tʃɛko bambino
Che un cieco bambino
that a blind child

kon bɔkːka di latːte si fatːʃa stimar
Con bocca di latte si faccia stimar!
with (a) mouth of milk himself should-make esteemed!

ma kwesto tiranːno
Ma questo tiranno
But this tyrant

kon barbaroiŋganːno
Con barbaro inganno
with barbarous deception

entrando per ʎːʎɔkːki mi fe sospirar
Entrando per gli occhi, mi fe' sospirar.
entering through [the] (my) eyes me made to-sigh.

Che fiero costume

Disdainful and ruthless

Poet unknown
English version by
James P. Dunn

Giovanni Legrenzi (1626-1690)
Edited by John Glenn Paton

Che fie - ro co-stu- me D'a-li - ge - ro nu-me, Che a for-za di pe - ne si fac-cia a-do -
Dis-dain-ful and ruth-less, The wing-ed god Cu-pid Com-pels us to love with his mis- siles of

rar, si fac-cia a-do- rar, Che a for-za di pe - ne si fac-cia a-do -
pain, his mis- siles of pain, Com-pels us to love with his mis - siles of

rar!_____ E pur nell' ar - do- re Il dio tra-di -
pain!_____ And so filled with pas- sion By his treach-'rous

Idiomatic translation : What a fierce custom Cupid has, who, by using punishment, makes himself adored!
Yet in my ardor the traitorous god

made me worship a lovely face.

What a cruel fate, that a blind child, scarcely weaned, should make himself esteemed! But this tyrant, with barbarous deception, entering through my eyes, made me sigh.

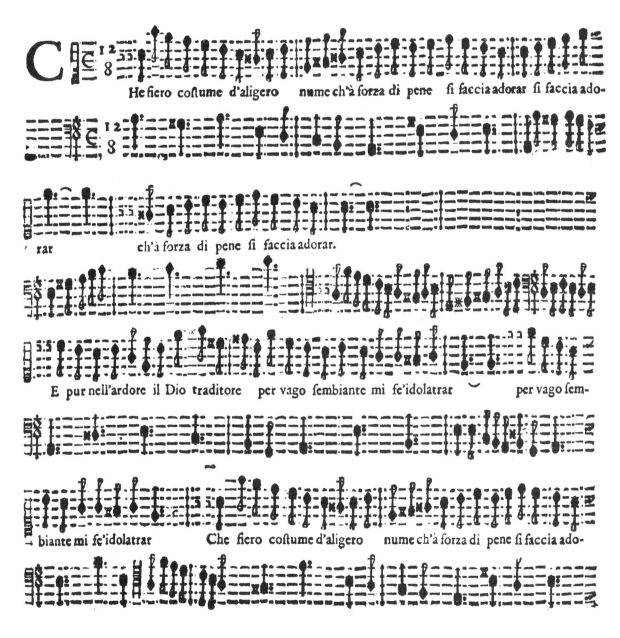

Che fiero costume

From *Echi di riverenza* by Giovanni Legrenzi. The voice part is in soprano clef; the continuo is in bass and tenor clefs. Notice the lack of punctuation in the text. Nearly all punctuation in modern editions has been added by editors.

5 "Tu lo sai"

Giuseppe Torelli
dʒuzɛp:pe torɛl:li

Poetic idea

"I really loved you; remember that!"

Background

Nothing is known about the origin of this lovely aria, but its composer was a violin virtuoso who contributed to the development of the solo violin concerto. These words were also set to music by Pietro Paolo Bencini (c1670-1755), found in Ms 5109, Biblioteca Casanatense, Rome.

Source

Bel Canto, edited by Albert Fuchs (Braunschweig: Litolff, 1901?). Fuchs stated that the arias in his collection were from the early 1700s and that they were not from operas. They were all to be found in the Royal Library in Dresden, which suffered serious damage in World War II. It is now called the Sächsische Landesbibliothek, but *"Tu lo sai"* is no longer there. Because the manuscript source is not available, the aria is printed here in Fuchs's arrangement. He presented it in Db major, which is probably not the original key, and with many expression markings in the late Romantic style. *Andantino* is also a tempo marking that was rare in Torelli's time.

tu   lo   sai   kwanto   tamai
Tu   lo   sai   quanto   t'amai,
You   [it]   know   how-much   you-I-loved,

tu   lo   sai   lo   sai   krudɛl
Tu   lo   sai,   lo   sai,   crudel!
You   [it]   know,   [it]   know,   cruel-one!

io   non   bramo   altra   merce
Io   non   bramo   altra   mercé,
I (do)   not   desire   other   compensation,

ma   rikɔrdati   di   me
Ma   ricordati   di   me,
but   remember   [-yourself of]   me,

e   pɔi   sprɛt:sa   un   infedel
E   poi   sprezza   un   infedel.
and   then   despise   an   unfaithful-one!

Tu lo sai

You know full well

Poet unknown
English version by
James P. Dunn

Giuseppe Torelli (1658-1709)
Edited by Albert Fuchs
Vocal Ornamentation by Arthur Schoep

Andantino, ♩ = 80 - 96

Tu lo_____ sai quan - to t'a - ma - i, Tu lo_____
You know__full well how much I love you, Ah, cruel_____

sai, lo sai cru - del! _____ Io non bra - mo
heart, how well you _____ know! _____ My de - sire, _____ no

cresc. dim.

al - tra mer - cè, Ma ri - cor - da - ti di me,
oth - er can be But that you think on - ly of me,

Idiomatic translation: You know how much I loved you, you know it, yes, you know it, cruel one! I do
not desire other compensation, but that you remember me

E poi sprez - za ___ un in - fe - del, E poi
And dis - dain ___ one ___ that is un - true, *And dis -*

sprez - za ___ un in - fe - del. Tu lo ___ sai
dain ___ one ___ that ___ is ___ un - true. *You know___ full well*

Quan - to ___ t'a ma - i, Tu lo ___ sai lo sai cru - del. ___
quan - to t'a - ma - i, *Tu lo ___ sai lo sai cru - del.*
how I do love you, *Ah, cruel ___ heart, how well ___ you know,*

and then despise an unfaithful one!

6 "Già il sole dal Gange"

from *L'Honestà negli amori*,
lonesta neʎ:ʎi amoɾi

Alessandro Scarlatti
ales:sandro skarlat:ti

Poetic idea

"How happy the whole world is at sunrise!" The person singing is Saldino, a pageboy, in the opera *Honesty in Love Affairs*. He is alone onstage, admiring the sunrise. The scene is Algeria in North Africa. *("Dal Gange"* is merely a figure of speech meaning the east.)

Background

Scarlatti was born in Palermo, Sicily, but he was sent to Rome at age 12 to study music. When he wrote this, his second opera, in 1680, he was 19 years old. He was already married and a father, and he had been appointed the music director to Queen Christina of Sweden, who lived in Rome.

The unique character of Roman society in the 1600s affected the creation of music there. The popes were the rulers of the Papal States; as guardians of public morality, some of them permitted theaters to operate, but others did not. Women almost never sang in public in Rome. Women could perform at private opera theaters maintained by wealthy persons, most of whom were relatives of popes and had received noble titles and important church posts.

This opera was sung for the first time in the palace of an exceptionally wealthy person who had no noble title, Giovanni Bernini (1598-1680). Bernini rose through his artistic talent and long service to many popes as a sculptor and architect. It is said that in his private theater Bernini designed the scenery, and he may have written the libretto of this opera. The preface to the libretto hints that the name, Felice Parnasso, which means "happy-one-who-has-reached-the-heights," was the pen name of someone famous.

dʒail sole dal gandʒe
Già il sole dal Gange
Already the sun from-the Ganges (the East)

pju kjaɾo sfavil:la
Più chiaro sfavilla
more brightly sparkles

e tɛrdʒeoɲ:ɲi stil:la
E terge ogni stilla
and dries every drop

del:lalba ke pjandʒe
Dell'alba che piange.
of-the-dawn, which weeps.

kol rad:ʒo doɾato
Col raggio dorato
With-the ray gilded

indʒɛm:maoɲ:ɲi stɛlo
Ingemma ogni stelo
it-adorns every blade

e ʎ:ʎastri del tʃɛlo
E gli astri del cielo
and the stars of-the sky

dipindʒe nel pɾato
Dipinge nel prato.
it-paints in-the field.

Sources

(1) *L'Honestà negl'Amori*, manuscript score of the opera in Biblioteca Estense, Modena, F.1057 (a 10-measure ritornello for string orchestra precedes each stanza); (2) *Arie*, manuscript collection, Biblioteca musicale governativa del Conservatorio di musica "S. Cecilia," Rome, A Ms 249. Both sources appear to be in the same handwriting. For voice (soprano clef) and continuo. Original key: A major.

The familiar edition was made by Parisotti in *Arie Antiche*, vol. 2 (Milan: Ricordi, 1890), when the singing of long runs was somewhat out of fashion with singers and audiences. In order to modernize Scarlatti's music, Parisotti used repeated words to break up the runs, a practice that others also used into the early 1900s. This destroyed the symbolism of the word "sun" rising on a scale, and emphasized the insignificant word "Ganges." The aria became popular, but in a false and inferior form.

Già il sole dal Gange

The sun from the Orient

Felice Parnasso
English version by
James P. Dunn

Alessandro Scarlatti (1660-1725)
Edited by John Glenn Paton

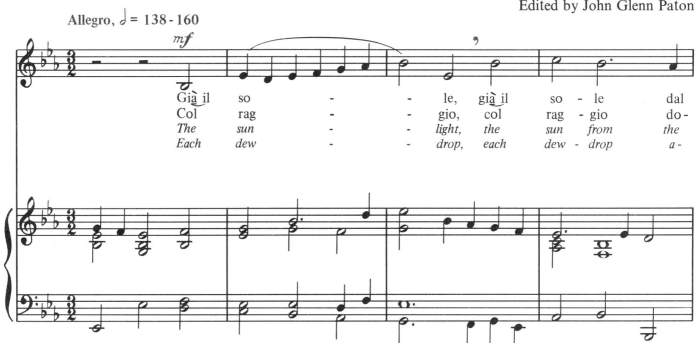

Idiomatic translation:
(First stanza:) Already the sun sparkles in the East
(Second stanza:) With a gilded ray

(1.) more brightly and dries every drop of the weeping dawn.
(2.) it adorns every blade of grass with dew, and it paints the stars of the sky in the field.

Gan - ge,   Già il so - - le, già il so - le dal
ra - to,   Col rag - - gio, col rag - gio do -
O - rient,   The sun - - light, the sun from the
glit - ter,   Each dew - - drop, each dew - drop a -

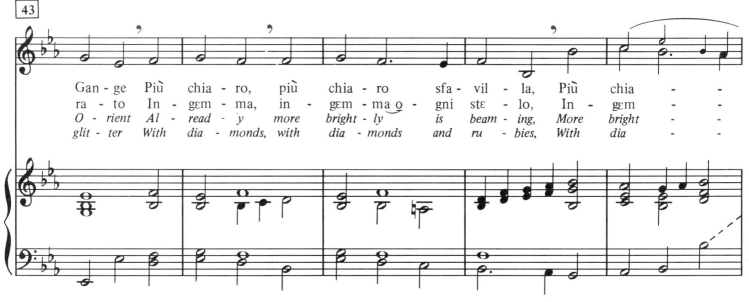

Gan - ge Più chia - ro, più chia - ro sfa - vil - la, Più chia - -
ra - to In - gɛm - ma, in - gɛm - ma o - gni stɛ - lo, In - gɛm -
O - rient Al - read - y more bright - ly is beam - ing, More bright -
glit - ter With dia - monds, with dia - monds and ru - bies, With dia -

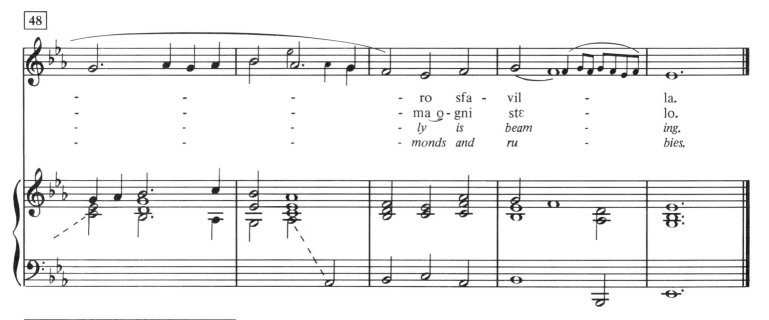

- ro sfa - vil - la.
- ma o - gni stɛ - lo.
- ly is beam - ing.
- monds and ru - bies.

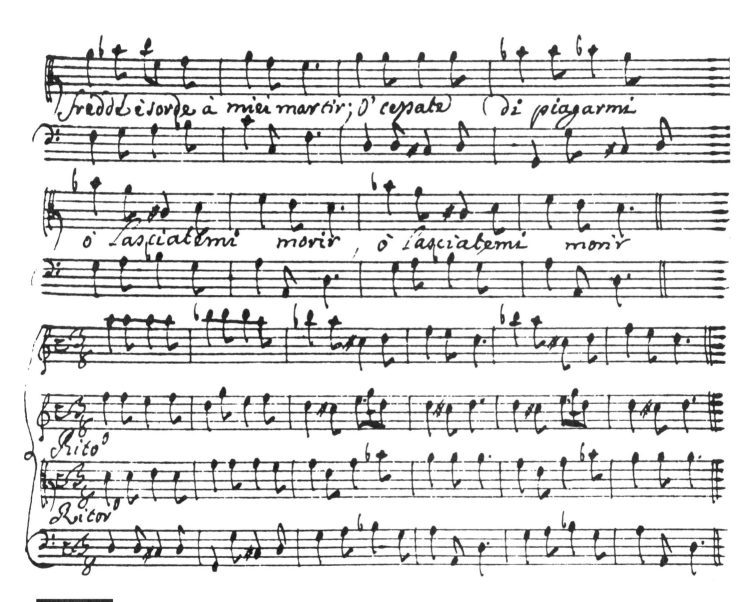

O cessate di piagarmi

A page from the manuscript score of Alessandro Scarlatti's *Pompeo* owned by the Royal Library, Brussels. This page shows the conclusion of the aria and the ritornello (postlude) for string instruments. The voice part is in alto clef, with middle C on the third line. Notice that the continuo part has no chord symbols to help the accompanist. This is the work of a professional music copyist; it is not Scarlatti's autograph.

"O cessate di piagarmi"

from *Pompeo*
pompɛo

Alessandro Scarlatti
ales:sandro skarlat:ti

Poetic idea

"Please stop being so hard on me. You do not show me love, but you could do so if you wanted to." Sesto, son of the Roman general, Pompey the Great, sings this to Issicratea, formerly the Queen of Pontus, now (about 15 B.C.) living under house arrest in Rome. Sesto loves Issicratea, but she is cold to him, still hoping to return to her husband and her homeland.

Background

Scarlatti was 22 years old when he wrote *Pompeo*, his fourth opera (1683). He was the music director to Queen Christina of Sweden, and this opera was performed in the private theater of the Colonna family. (For more about Scarlatti's life read the notes to his other arias.)

Except for a few romantic comedies in exotic settings, the stories of Scarlatti's operas all come out of ancient Roman history. His noble patrons wanted idealized stories about persons of nobility caught in rivalries of love and conflicts between love and duty.

Musically, Scarlatti's operas consisted of recitatives and arias. Recitatives are sung in irregular rhythms like those of speech, and they are used to carry on conversations and deliver information. Arias have regular dance-like rhythms, and they are used for characters in the opera to express their personal emotions in arias.

Source

Pompeo, Act 2, scene 5. Score in the Bibliothèque royale Albert Ier., Brussels, MS II 3962. For voice (alto clef, beginning on a1) and continuo, with an interlude for string quartet. Original key: D minor. Meter: 3/8 [sic]. Photo- reproduction in *Handel Sources*, Vol. 6 (New York: Garland, 1986). Handel knew this opera and borrowed parts of ten arias (but not this one) to use in his own music.

Ritornello means an instrumental interlude that is played between stanzas and at the end.

The familiar version, edited by Parisotti in *Arie Antiche*, vol. 1 (Milan: Ricordi, 1885), omits the introduction, the ritornello, and the second stanza. In this aria the repeated melodic tones symbolize fascination, while the moving bass part conveys emotional restlessness. Parisotti's numerous musical alterations reverse the symbolism: They increase melodic movement in the voice part and decrease it in the bass.

o tʃes:sate di pjagarmi
O cessate di piagarmi,
O cease [of] to-wound-me,

o laʃatemi morir
O lasciatemi morir!
o let-me die,

lutʃingrate
Luci ingrate,
eyes ungrateful,

dispjetate
Dispietate,
pitiless,

pju di dʒɛloe pju de marmi
Più di gelo e più de' marmi
more of ice and more of marble

fred:de sordea mjɛi martir
Fredde e sorde a miei martir!
cold and deaf to my tortures.

pju dun angwe pju dun aspe
Più d'un angue, più d'un aspe
More than-a serpent, more than-an asp,

krudie sordia mjɛi sospir
Crudi e sordi a' miei sospir,
cruel and deaf to my sighs,

ɔk:kialtɛri
Occhi alteri,
eyes proud,

tʃɛkie fjɛri
Ciechi e fieri,
blind and cruel,

voi potete risanarmi
Voi potete risanarmi,
you can again-heal-me,

e godeteal mio langwir
E godete al mio languir.
and you-enjoy [at-the] my languishing.

O cessate di piagarmi

O relent, no more torment me

Nicola Minato
English version by
James P. Dunn

Alessandro Scarlatti (1660-1725)
Vocal ornamentation by Arthur Schoep
Realization by John Glenn Paton

Idiomatic translations:
(First stanza) O cease to wound me, O let me die.
(Second stanza) More than a serpent, more than an asp, cruel and deaf to my sighing,

9

𝄐 la - scia - te - mi mo - rir! Lu - c'in - gra - te,
Cru - di e sor - di a miei sos - pir. Oc - chi al - te - ri,
O,   I pray   you, let   me   die!   Eyes   un - grate - ful,
Harsh and heed - less   to   my sighs!   Eyes   so   bane - ful

12

di - spie - ta - te, Lu - c'in - gra - te, di - spie - ta - te,
cie - chi e fie - ri, Oc - chi al - te - ri, cie - chi e fie - ri,
spite - ful, hate - ful, Eyes   un - grate - ful, spite - ful, hate - ful,
and   dis - dain - ful, Eyes   so   bane - ful and   dis - dain - ful,

15

cresc.   *f*

Più di ge - lo e più de' mar - mi Fred - de e sor - de a
Voi po - te - te ri - sa - nar - mi, E go - de - te al
Cold   as   ice   and cold as mar - ble, Cold   and deaf to   my
You   can ease   me,   heal   and cleanse me, Yet   you   joy   in   my

(1.) Ungrateful, pitiless eyes, colder than ice and colder than marble, cold and deaf to my torture.
(2.) proud eyes, so blind and fierce, you are able to heal me again, but you enjoy seeing me languish.

"Sento nel core"

Alessandro Scarlatti
ales:sandro skarlat:ti

Poetic idea

"Something is bothering me; maybe I'm falling in love!"

Background

Throughout his long career, Alessandro Scarlatti composed *cantate da camera*, "chamber cantatas." There were no concert halls such as we have today, but Italians categorized music according to the place of performance: operas for the theater, Latin sacred music for the church, and chamber music for private homes. Cantata was the name often given to music for one or more voices with instrumental accompaniment.

Most cantatas were unpublished and were preserved only in handwritten books made by professional copyists. These books were treasured possessions of the wealthy, used by the singers they employed. Many such books survive today in European libraries.

Scarlatti composed over 600 cantatas, noteworthy for their ingenuity and variety in dealing with the unchanging subject of romantic love. "Sento nel core" is one of the simplest, consisting of two arias separated by a recitative. In the recitative the lover speaks to the beloved, expressing fear and uncertainty about falling in love. The final aria says "I fear falling in love, but I feel that I shall love you."

Sources

(1) Manuscript, Additional 31,512, British Library, London; (2) Manuscript, Noseda L.22-24, Library of Conservatorio di Musica Giuseppe Verdi, Milan; (3) Manuscript, uncatalogued, University of Aberystwyth, Wales, as reproduced in *The Italian Cantata*, vol. 13 (New York: Garland, 1986). Original key: E minor in sources (1) and (3), C minor in (2).

sento nel kɔre
Sento nel core
I-feel in[-the] (my) heart

tʃɛrto dolore
Certo dolore,
(a) certain pain

ke la mia patʃe
Che la mia pace
which [the] my peace

turbando va
Turbando va.
disturbing goes.

splɛndeuna fatʃe
Splende una face
(There) shines a torch

ke lalmat:ʃɛnde
Che l'alma accende,
which the-soul inflames;

se non ɛamore
Se non è amore,
if not it-is love,

amor saɾa
Amor sarà.
love it-will-be.

The familiar edition has incorrect slurs. In the 1600s it was common to place a weak syllable on a quick note slurred to a longer note, as in m6. Most modern editors reject such rhythms as being awkward, but if performed with lightness and grace, they can be charming.

Sento nel core

Sorrow unending

Poet unknown
English version by
James P.Dunn

Alessandro Scarlatti (1660-1725)
Vocal Ornamentation and Arrangement by
Arthur Schoep

Idiomatic translation: In my heart I feel a certain pain which disturbs my peace.

A torch shines which kindles my soul. If it is not love, it will become love.

Se non è a - mo - re, _____ A - mor _____ sa - rà.
If not true lov - ing, _____ then _____ soon _____ will be.

Sɛn - to nel cɔ - re _____ Cɛr - to do - lo - re, Cɛr - to do -
Sor - row un end - ing, _____ My heart tor - ment - ing, My heart tor -

lo - re, Che la mia pa - ce _____ Tur ban - do _____ va,
ment - ing, All peace pre vent - ing, _____ No rest _____ for _____ me!

"Le Violette"

from *Pirro e Demetrio*
pir:ro e demɛtrjo

Alessandro Scarlatti
ales:sandro skarlat:ti

Poetic idea

"Have you tiny violets been put here as a message for me? Am I aiming too high in loving such a wonderful person?" The person who sings this is a youth named Mario in the opera *Pyrrhus and Demetrius*. He is alone in a garden, thinking about his love for a woman who is nobly born.

Background

After his youthful successes in Rome, Scarlatti moved to Naples, which was under Spanish rule, and became the musical director to the Spanish viceroy. His appointment included directing the leading opera theater with a permanent company of nine singers and five instrumentalists. *Pirro e Demetrio* (1694) was among Scarlatti's most successful operas. It was performed in many cities, even in London, but the numerous performances brought the composer no additional payment.

The interweaving of the voice and violin parts in this aria is typical of Scarlatti's mature operas, some of which contain no continuo arias.

Sources

(1) *Pirro e Demetrio*, manuscript score of the opera in Biblioteca del Conservatorio di Musica San Pietro a Majella, Rari 7.1.11. (Microfilm courtesy of Prof. Karl Kroeger, Music Library, University of Colorado at Boulder.) Scored for voice (soprano clef, starting on a2), violins *"tutti all'unisono"*, and continuo. Key: A. (2) *Songs in the new opera call'd Pyrrhus and Demetrius* (London: Walsh, 1709?). Copy in the Clark Library, University of California at Los Angeles. English text only. Violin part omitted. Voice and continuo parts exactly duplicate those in the Naples score, except for one interesting variation: m32 is altered to minor

rudʒadoze
Rugiadose,
Dewy,

odoroze
Odorose
fragrant

violet:te gratsioze
Violette graziose,
violets   graceful,

voi vi   state
Voi vi   state
you there stand

vergoɲ:ɲoze
Vergognose,
modest,

(c-naturals instead of c-sharps in A Major).

A libretto published for the London production in 1709, in which the role of Mario was sung by a woman, gives this singable translation:

Blushing violets,
Sweetly smelling,
From your verdant fragrant dwelling,
You upbraid me
For aspiring
And admiring
Those above me,
Tho' they love me;
And deride me
With too much Ambition swelling.

The familiar version, made by an anonymous editor, omits m4-m11 and omits or alters other passages. Having shortened the aria drastically, the editor lengthened it overall with a long repetition beginning with *"Voi vi state vergognose."* This extension is furnished with ornaments, which are acceptable but are certainly not from Scarlatti.

mɛd:zoaskoze
Mezzo ascose
half   hidden

fra   le   fɔʎ:ʎe
Fra   le   foglie,
among the leaves

e   zgridate
E   sgridate
and you-rebuke

le   mie vɔʎ:ʎe
Le   mie voglie,
[the] my desires,

ke   son trɔp:po ambitsioze
Che   son troppo ambiziose.
which are too   ambitious.

Le Violette

The Violets

Adriano Morselli
English version by
James P. Dunn

Alessandro Scarlatti (1660-1725)
Edited by John Glenn Paton

Allegretto, ♩ = 72 - 88

Note: Treble notes with upward stems are played by unison violins in the original. Treble notes with downward stems are part of the realization supplied by the editor.

Ru-gia-do - se, O - do - ro - se,
Ten-der vio - let, I a - dore you,

Ru-gia-do-se, O-do-ro-se, Vi - o - let - te Gra-zi -
Ten-der vio - let, I a - dore you, O how bash - ful, Gent - ly

o - se, Vi - o - let - te Gra-zi - o - se, Voi vi sta-te Ver-go -
grace - ful, O how bash - ful, Gent - ly grace - ful, How you shrink from My ad -

Idiomatic translation: Dewy, fragrant, graceful violets, you stand there modestly,

half hidden among the leaves, and you rebuke my desires, which are too ambitious.

Le mie vo - glie,
Are my wish - es,

Che_ son trɔp - po, son
You_ re - buke, yes, re-

trɔp - po am - bi - zio - se._
buke my ar - dent glanc - es._

Ru-gia-
Ten-der

do - se, O - do - ro - se,
vio - let, I a - dore you,

Vi - o -
O how

let - te gra - zi - o - se,
bash - ful, gent - ly grace - ful,

Ru - gia -
*Ten - der_*

"Se Florinda è fedele"

from *La donna ancora è fedele*
la dɔn:na aŋkora ɛ fedele

Alessandro Scarlatti
ales:sandro skarlat:ti

Poetic idea

"Shall I let myself fall in love? The usual ways of wooing don't impress me, but faithfulness will win me." The singer is Alidoro, who has just overheard a conversation in which he learned that Florinda is in love with him. (If a woman sings this aria, the name can be changed to Florindo; no other changes are needed.)

Background

The Lady Still Is Faithful (1698) is another of the operas that Scarlatti composed for Naples during his years of great productivity there. As in the preceding aria, the interplay of violin and voice is typical of Scarlatti's mature style.

After 1702, political unrest caused Scarlatti to seek positions in Florence and Rome. He later returned to Naples as an employee of the Austrian viceroy. He composed even during the years of semi-retirement before his death in Naples. His son, Domenico, born in the same year as J. S. Bach, became one of the leading composers

se florinda ɛ fedele
Se Florinda è fedele,
If Florinda is faithful,

io min:namorerɔ
Io m'innamorerò.
I [myself-]will-fall-in-love.

potra ben larko tɛndere
Potrà ben l'arco tendere
Will-be-able well the-bow to-draw

il faretrato artʃɛr
Il faretrato arcier,
the quivered archer,

kio mi saprɔ difɛndere
Ch'io mi saprò difendere
For-I myself will-know-how to-defend

of keyboard music of all time.

Source

La Donna ancora è fedele, manuscript score of the opera in Biblioteca del Conservatorio di Musica San Pietro a Majella, Naples, Rari 7.I.3. For violins in unison, voice (soprano clef), and

daun gwardo luziŋgjɛr
Da un guardo lusinghier.
from a glance flattering.

prɛgi pjanti e kwerɛle
Preghi, pianti e querele
pleas, tears and laments

io non askolterɔ
Io non ascolterò,
I not will-hear,

ma se sara fedele
Ma se sarà fedele,
but if (she-)will-be faithful,

io min:namorerɔ
Io m'innamorerò.
I [myself-]will-fall-in-love.

continuo. Key: C major. Meter: 3/8.

The familiar version, which uses the masculine form of the beloved's name, was published by Parisotti in 1885. Ludwig Landshoff published an authentic edition, with violin obbligato, in *Alte Meister des Bel Canto* (Leipzig: Peters, 1915).

Se Florinda è fedele

If Florinda be constant

Domenico Filippo Contini
English version by
James P. Dunn

Alessandro Scarlatti (1670-1725)
Vocal Ornamentation by Arthur Schoep
Realization by John Glenn Paton

Note: Treble notes with upward stems are played by unison violins in the original. Treble notes with downward stems are part of the realization supplied by the editor.

Idiomatic translation: If Florinda is faithful, I shall fall in love with her.

24

Io m'in - na - mo - re - rò, S'è__ fe - de - le__ Flo - rin - da, m'in -
Sure - ly I'll fall in_____ love, I__ will fall in_____ love, I'll sure -

29

na - mo - re - rò, m'in-na- mo-re - rò, m'in-na- mo-re -
ly__ fall in love, I will fall in love, I will fall in

34

rò,_____ Io m'in - na - mo - re - rò.
love,_____ I'll sure - ly__ fall in love.

40

Po - trà ben l'ar - co ten - de - re Il fa - re -
Sir Cu - pid with his dart and bow, So clev - er,__

Cupid can well draw his bow,

but I shall know how to defend myself from a flattering glance. Pleas, tears, and laments
I will not listen to, but if she will be faithful, I shall fall in love.

"Star vicino"

Composer Unknown

Poetic idea

"I love being near you, I hate being away from you."

Background

It used to be believed that this song was composed by a famous Roman painter, Salvator Rosa (1615–1673). In fact, Rosa owned a hand-written book of songs; he had written the words to three of them. Long after Rosa's death, the book was sold to a British traveler, Dr. Charles Burney, who believed that Rosa had composed all of the poetry and all of the music in the book.

In *A General History of Music*, Burney described Rosa's book and printed musical excerpts from it. When Burney's history became famous, the excerpts were arranged and published as solo songs, spreading the myth that Rosa had been a composer. Although musical scholars suspected that this was not true, the idea of a painter-composer appealed to many musicians of the Romantic era. Franz Liszt even wrote a piano piece, *"Canzonetta di Salvator Rosa,"* based on one of the songs, *"Vado ben spesso."*

In 1949 Frank Walker, an English musicologist, examined Rosa's book and determined that Rosa actually composed none of the music attributed to him. The first twelve pieces in the book, all in one person's handwriting, are known from other sources to be works of well-known composers. The other pieces were copied by other persons onto blank pages in the book after Rosa's death. No. 15 is an aria that Alessandro Scarlatti composed in 1681. *"Vado ben spesso,"* now known to be a composition of Giovanni Bononcini, is no. 19.

"Star vicino" is no. 21; it was certainly copied into the book at least eight years after Rosa's death. Dr. Walker reported that *"Star vicino"* is a da capo aria with a middle section that begins *"Altre gioie"* ("Other joys"). Unfortunately, the missing section has never been published.

The Rosa book was sold to a French musicologist, Genevieve Thibault. Since her death, the book has been unavailable to scholars and remains so as this is written.

Source

Charles Burney, *A General History of Music*, Vol. 4 (London: 1789). For voice and continuo. Original key: F major. This edition presents Burney's excerpt, m1–m16, followed by a second stanza based on versions from the 1800s. The text of the second stanza is by Count Pepoli of Bologna, and an anonymous editor added the final eight measures.

Bibliography

Frank Walker, "Salvator Rosa and Music," *Monthly Musical Record*, October 1949. Mr. Albi Rosenthal, London, confirmed the later ownership of the Rosa book.

star	vitʃinoal	bɛl:lidol	ke	sama
Star	**vicino al**	**bell'idol**	**che**	**s'ama**
To-be	near to-the	beautiful-idol	that	one-loves

ɛil	pju	vago	dilɛt:to	damor
È il	**piu**	**vago**	**diletto**	**d'amor.**
is the	most	attractive	joy	of-love.

star	lontano dal	bɛn	ke	si	brama
Star	**lontano dal**	**ben**	**che**	**si**	**brama,**
To-be	far from-the	beloved	whom	one	desires

ɛ	damoreil	pju	vivo	dolor
È	**d'amore il**	**più**	**vivo**	**dolor.**
is	of-love	the most	vital	sorrow.

Star vicino

To be near one's beloved

Poet unknown
English version by
James P. Dunn

Composer unknown
Vocal Ornamentation and Arrangement
(second stanza) by Arthur Schoep

Moderato, ♩ = 108 - 120

Star vi - ci - no al bel - l'i - dol che s'a - ma,
To be near one's be - lov - ed, fair beau - ty

È il più va - go di - let - to___ d'a - mor,
Is love's pleas - ure, love's joy and___ de - light,

È il più va - - - - - -
Is love's pleas - - - - - -

Idiomatic translation: To be near the beautiful idol one loves is the most attractive joy of love.

- - - - go di - lɛt - to d'a - mor!
- - - - ure, love's joy and de - light!

Star lon - ta - no dal bɛn che si bra - ma,
But to long from a - far for one's dear - est,

Ɛ d'a - mo - re il più vi - vo__ do - lor,
Is to suf - fer in deep - est__ de - spair,

Ɛ d'a
Ah, the

To be far from her whom one desires is the greatest sorrow of love!

"Pur dicesti, o bocca bella"

Antonio Lotti
anˈtɔnjo ˈlɔt:ti

Poetic idea

"You have just said yes to my love, after I kissed you, and I am so happy!"

Background

Lotti sang as a choirboy under Legrenzi's direction at St. Mark's Cathedral in Venice; later in life he became the music director there. He also wrote about 30 operas and many cantatas, but the origin of this aria is not known.

Source

Les Gloires de l'Italie, edited by Francois Auguste Gevaert (Paris: private subscription, 1868). Key: E major. Gevaert used a manuscript from a private collection, present whereabouts unknown.

Gevaert presented the authentic voice part and a keyboard realization; he also used separate lines to present the continuo part (which is identical to the lowest notes of the keyboard part) and suggested vocal ornaments.

Parisotti borrowed nine of Gevaert's editions for his *Arie Antiche*. In copying this aria, Parisotti added more ornaments, and in some cases he omitted the original notes and replaced them with Gevaert's ornaments. In this edition, Parisotti's changes have been eliminated. All cue-sized notes are Gevaert's ornaments. Knowing which notes are original gives the singer freedom to accept the ornaments, alter them, or ignore them.

pur ditˈʃesti o ˈbok:ka ˈbɛl:la
Pur dicesti, o bocca bella,
Yet you-said, O mouth beautiful,

kwel soˈave ˈkaro si
Quel soave e caro sì,
that sweet and dear "yes,"

ke fa ˈtut:toil mio pjatˈʃer
Che fa tutto il mio piacer.
which makes all [the] my pleasure.

per oˈnor di ˈsua fatˈʃɛl:la
Per onor di sua facella
For honor of his [torch] (reputation),

kon un ˈbatʃo aˈmor taˈpri
Con un bacio Amor t'aprì,
with a kiss Love you-opened,

ˈdoltʃe ˈfonte del goˈder
Dolce fonte del goder.
sweet fountain of[-the] pleasure.

---

66 ■ *26 Italian Songs and Arias*

Pur dicesti, o bocca bella

Gently murmur

Poet unknown
English version by
James P. Dunn

Antonio Lotti (ca. 1667-1740)
Vocal Ornamentation and Arrangement by
François Auguste Gevaert

Idiomatic translation: O beautiful mouth, you said that sweet and dear word, "yes,"

Che fa___ tut - to il mio pia - cer, il mio pia - cer.
Fill - ing___ hap - py___ hours with joy, my hours with joy.

Pur di - ce - sti, o boc - ca, boc - ca
Gen - tly___ mur - mur, your lips all sweet and

Quel___ so - a___ ve e ca___ ro

bɛl - la, o boc - ca, boc - ca bɛl - la, Quel so - a - ve e ca - ro___
ten - der, your lips all sweet and ten - der, Ca - dence___ soft, so___ dear to___

ten.   *ten.*   *ten.*

which makes all my pleasure.

For the honor of his reputation,

Love opened you with a kiss, sweet fountain of pleasure.

"Non posso disperar"

from *Eraclea*
eraklɛa

Giovanni Bononcini
dʒovan:ni bonontʃini

Poetic idea

"You have told me that you do not love me, but I cannot give up now." The person who sings this is King Romulus of Rome, who is in love with a Sabine noblewoman, Ericlea. Legend tells that when the early Romans had a shortage of women, they abducted the women from a neighboring tribe, the Sabines. Ericlea is one of these, and King Romulus hopes that she can learn to love him in spite of being his prisoner.

Background

Bononcini, a young man from Modena, arrived in Rome during the reign of a tolerant pope, when the famous Tordinona Theater was operating. For his debut in Rome he provided additional arias that were sung in an already existing opera: *"Non posso disperar"* was sung in *Eraclea* by Antonio Draghi. The Tordinona closed soon afterward, but Bononcini found work in a noble Roman household.

This aria confirms a modern scholar's statement that 'harmonically, Bononcini was a bold innovator, and his music is spiced with unusual dissonances and rapid modulations which horrified many of his contemporaries." (H. C. Wolff, *New Oxford History of Music*, v5, p75.)

Sources

There are three manuscript sources for this aria, all in the handwriting of the same professional copyist: (1) *Arie della commedia del ratto delle sabbine*, Barberini latini 4161, Biblioteca apostolica vaticana, Vatican City; (2) no title, Barberini latini 4164, same library; and (3) no title, G392, Biblioteca musicale governativa del Conservatorio de Musica "S. Cecilia." For voice (soprano clef) and continuo. Original key: G minor with one flat.

non pɔs:so dispeɾaɾ
Non posso disperar!
Not I-can despair!

sɛi trɔp:po kaɾal kɔr
Sei troppo cara al cor.
You-are too dear to[-the] (my) heart.

il sↄlo speɾaɾe
Il solo sperare
The only hope

davɛɾ a dʒoiɾe
D'aver a gioire
of-having to be-happy

mɛun doltʃe laŋgwiɾe
M'è un dolce languire,
to-me-is a sweet languishing,

mɛun kaɾo dolↄɾ
M'è un caro dolor.
to-me-is a dear pain.

Sources (1) and (2) both confirm that the composer was Bononcini. Source (3), which names no composer, was edited by Parisotti in *Arie Antiche*, vol. 2 (Milan: Ricordi, 1890). He took a wrong guess and named the composer as Severo de Luca, who composed other arias in source (3). The familiar edition, therefore, gives the wrong composer's name; it also uses bombastic fortissimos and inserts incorrect accidentals into m31 and m32. Bononcini's use of a quickly fleeting Neapolitan harmony is authentic and is typical of his style.

Non posso disperar

Nor must I now despair

Silvio Stampiglia
English version by
James P. Dunn

Giovanni Bononcini (1670-1747)
Vocal Ornamentation by Arthur Schoep
Realization by John Glenn Paton

Idiomatic translation: I cannot despair, you are too dear to my heart.

rar, Sɛi trɔp - po ca - ra, sɛi trɔp - po ca - ra al cɔr, Non pɔs - so_ di - spe-
spair, You're far___ too pre - cious, too pre - cious to my heart, Nor must___ I __ now de-

rar, Sɛi trɔp - po ca - ra,
spair, You're far___ too_pre - cious,

Sɛi trɔp - po, trɔp - po_
For you are far too__

ca - ra, ca - ra_al cɔr,
pre - cious to my heart,

Sɛi trɔp - po, trɔp - po_
For you are far too__

ca - ra, ca - ra_al cɔr.
pre - cious to my heart.

The only hope of happiness for me is a sweet languishment, a dear pain.

ra, sɛi trɔp - po ca - ra al cɔr. Non pɔs - so di - spe - rar, Sɛi trɔp - po ca -
cious, too pre - cious to my heart. Nor must I now de - spair, You're far too pre -

ra,
cious,

Sɛi trɔp - po, trɔp - po ca - ra, ca - ra al
For you are far too pre - cious to my

cɔr,
heart,

Sɛi trɔp - po, trɔp - po ca - ra, ca - ra al
For you are far too pre - cious to my

cɔr!
heart!

"Per la gloria d'adorarvi"

from *Griselda*
grizᴇlda

Giovanni Bononcini
dʒovaⁿːni bonontʃini

Poetic idea

"I will love you even if I have no hope of your loving me in return!" The person who sings the aria is Ernesto in the opera *Griselda*.

Background

Please read about Bononcini in the notes to the preceding aria. Bononcini's tuneful operas brought him success in other capital cities as well. *Griselda*, the most popular opera of his career, was composed for London in 1722. Italian opera was in vogue, and Bononcini's operas outsold those of his competitor, George Frideric Handel.

Sources

Griselda, full score of the opera, (London: Walsh, 1722?) copy in the British Library, London. For voice (treble clef), violin and figured bass. Original key: F major. Original tempo: *Andante* (Italian for "going" or "walking"). Each section of the aria is printed only once, with repeat signs. In the score, the instrumental introduction is repeated at the end of the aria, as a postlude. Omit m81 if the postlude is played.

The familiar edition alters the slurs that Bononcini wrote and gives him a spurious middle name, "Battista." Note that the appoggiatura in m12 and similar passages are original; they are to be performed as eighth-notes or as quarter-notes and accented.

per la glɔrja dadorᴀrvi
Per la gloria d'adorarvi
For the glory of-adoring-you

vɔʎːʎo amᴀrvio lutʃi kᴀre
Voglio amarvi, o luci care:
I-want to-love-you, o eyes dear.

amᴀndo penerɔ
Amando penerò
Loving, I-will-suffer,

ma sᴇmpre vamerɔ
Ma sempre v'amerò,
but always you-I-will-love,

si si nel mio penᴀre
Sì, sì, nel mio penare:
yes, yes, in[-the] my suffering,

kᴀre kᴀre
Care, care.
dear-ones, dear-ones.

sᴇntsa spᴇme di dilᴇtːto
Senza speme di diletto
Without hope of pleasure

vᴀno afːfᴇtːto e sospirᴀre
Vano affetto e sospirare,
vain affection it-is to-sigh,

ma i vᴏstri dᴏltʃi rᴀi
Ma i vostri dolci rai
but [the] your sweet [rays] glances

ki vagedːʒar pwɔ mᴀi
Chi vagheggiar può mai,
who admire can ever

e non vamᴀre
E non v'amare?
and not you-love?

Per la gloria d'adorarvi

For the sheer delight of loving

Paolo Antonio Rolli
English version by
James P. Dunn

Giovanni Bononcini (1670-1747)
Edited by John Glenn Paton
Vocal Ornamentation by Arthur Schoep

Idiomatic translation: For the glory of adoring you, I want to love you, O dear eyes.

Loving you, I will suffer, yet I will love you always, yes, in my suffering, dear, dear eyes.

Pe - ne - rò, v'a - me - rò, Ca - re, ca - re.
Love   and pain,   tho'   in vain,   I   a - dore   you.

Pe - ne - rò, v'a - me - rò, Ca - re, ca - re.
Love   and pain,   tho'   in vain,   I   a - dore   you.

Without hope of pleasure, it is a vain affection to sigh.

But your sweet glances! who can admire them and not love you?

"Sebben, crudele"

from *La costanza in amor vince l'inganno*
la kostantsa in amor vintʃe liŋgan:no

Antonio Caldara
antɔnjo kaldara

Poetic idea

"I will go on loving you until my persistence makes you love me." The singer is Aminta, a shepherd, who is puzzled by the unresponsive behavior of Silvia, a shepherdess, who used to love him.

Background

Like Antonio Lotti, Caldara was a choirboy at St. Mark's Basilica in Venice under the direction of Giovanni Legrenzi. In 1710 Caldara wrote *Faithfulness in Love Defeats Treachery* for the public theater at Macerata. He was the music director of a princely household in Rome, where the opera was repeated the next year. The moralistic title assured the audience no religious person would be offended by the story.

In 1716 Caldara moved to Austria to serve the Imperial Court in Vienna. There he composed new music to the libretto of this opera. Entitled *Opera Pastorale*, it includes an aria, *"Sebben crudele,"* but with a different melody.

Sources

(1) *La costanza in amor vince l'inganno*, manuscript score of the opera, Biblioteca musicale governativa del Conservatorio di Musica "S. Cecilia," Rome, G ms 184. In Act I, scene 3. For voice (tenor clef), two violins, viola and continuo (the upper strings play only when the voice is silent). Original key: E minor; (2) Libretto for the 1711 performance, same library, Libretto XII.13.

The essential parts of this aria consist of 30 measures of vocal music, which are repeated in various ways, by the voice and by the instruments, to form a full-length aria. With all of its repetitions, the original is 160 measures long. This edition omits some repetitions, shortening the aria to 94 measures; nothing essential is left out.

The familiar version was edited by Parisotti in *Arie Antiche*, Vol. 1 (Milan: Ricordi, 1885). He used an eighth-note pulse throughout, lessening the minuet character of the aria.

seb:bɛn krudɛle
Sebben, crudele,
Although, cruel one,

mi fai laŋgwir
Mi fai languir,
me you-make languish,

sɛmpre fedɛle
Sempre fedele
always faithful,

ti vɔʎ:ʎoamar
Ti voglio amar.
you I-want to-love.

kon la luŋget:tsa
Con la lunghezza
With the length

del mio servir
Del mio servir
of[-the] my servitude

la tua fjerɛt:tsa
La tua fierezza
[the] your pride

saprɔ staŋkar
Saprò stancar.
I-will-know-how to-wear-down.

Sebben, crudele

Savage and heartless is your cruel scorn

Poet unknown
English version by
James P. Dunn

Antonio Caldara (ca. 1670-1736)
Vocal Ornamentation by Arthur Schoep
Realization by John Glenn Paton

*Idiomatic translation:*Cruel one, although you make me languish.

I want to love you faithfully always.

Seb - ben, cru - de - le, Mi fai lan - guir,_____
Sav - age and heart - less Is your cruel scorn,_____

Sem - pre___ fe - de - le Ti vo - glio a - mar.
Faith - ful___ and___ daunt - less Is ___ my love in turn.

Con la lun - ghez - za
Your slave for - ev - er,

Del mi - o ser - vir La tua fie - rez - za, la tua fie -
Each wish___ I'd___ serve, For - swear - ing nev - er, for - swear - ing

With the persistence of my servitude, I will know how to wear down your pride.

*In the original, m39-m42 are repeated.

"Alma del core"

from *La costanza in amor vince l'inganno*

Antonio Caldara
antɔnjo kaldara

Poetic idea

"I shall always love you faithfully, being happy as long as I can kiss you." The singer is Clizia, declaring her love for Tirsi, who immediately returns her promise to be faithful.

Background

Please read the notes about *"Sebben crudele,"* which comes earlier in the same opera.

Source

Same as for *"Sebben crudele"*. From Act I, scene 20. For voice (soprano clef) and continuo. (There is a 16-measure introduction for four-part strings; only the first two measures of it are included in this edition.) Original key: A major with two sharps.

Following *"Alma del core,"* the aria is repeated in a D-major version by Tirsi. The first four measures of the voice part are omitted so that the aria begins with the continuo playing at m7. Tirsi, whose part is in alto clef, sings the following text:

Dolce mia vita, cor del mio seno,
Sempre quest'alma t'adorerà.
Al tuo splendore questo mio core
Clizia fedele s'aggirerà.

The printed libretto of the Roman performance in 1711 does not contain *"Alma del core"*.

The familiar version of the aria was edited by Ludwig Landshoff in *Alte Meister des Bel Canto* (Leipzig: Peters, 1914). A responsible editor, Landshoff described his sources in detail, but the publisher has dropped that information from recent printings.

alma del kɔre
Alma del core,
Soul of[-the] (my) heart,

spirto del:lalma
Spirto dell'alma,
spirit of[-the] (my) soul,

sempre kostante tadorerɔ
Sempre costante t'adorerò!
always constant, you-I-will-adore.

sarɔ kontento
Sarò contento
I-shall-be happy

nel mio tormento
Nel mio tormento
in[-the] my torment

se kwel bɛl lab:bro batʃar potrɔ
Se quel bel labbro baciar potrò.
if that beautiful lip to-kiss I-will-be-able.

Alma del core

Spirit of being

Poet unknown
English version by
James P. Dunn

Antonio Caldara (ca. 1670-1736)
Vocal Ornamentation by Arthur Schoep
Realization by John Glenn Paton

Idiomatic translation: Soul of my heart, spirit of my soul, always constant,
I will adore you.

I shall be happy in my torment if I can kiss those beautiful lips.

Al - ma del co - re, Spir - to dell' al - ma,
Spir - it of be - ing, Soul of my spir - it,

Sɛm - pre co - stan - te t'a - do - re - rò,
Ev - er un - fail - ing my love shall be,

Sɛm - pre co - stan - te t'a - do - re - rò.
Ev - er un - fail - ing my love shall be.

"Come raggio di sol"

Antonio Caldara
antɔnjo kaldara

Poetic idea

"A cheerful smile may hide a grieving heart."

Background

Nothing is known about the origin of this song, which appeared in published collections in the 1800s. Caldara was a prolific composer. Until his music has been completely researched, one cannot say with certainty whether this is a genuine composition of Caldara's or a Romantic period forgery.

Source

Gemme d'antichità, No. 77, edited by "L.P." (London: Lonsdale, between 1863 and 1878). For voice and piano. Key: E minor. The sixth line of text reads: *"...di gioia un'alma infiora"*. The many expression markings reflect a late Romantic style of performance. This edition removes some of the extremes, but no authority is claimed.

kome rad:ʒo di sol mite sereno
Come raggio di sol mite e sereno
As (a) ray of sun mild and serene,

sovra platʃidi flut:ti si ripɔza
Sovra placidi flutti si riposa,
upon placid waves [itself] rests,

mentre del mare nel profondo seno
Mentre del mare nel profondo seno
while of-the sea in-the profound bosom

sta la tempesta askoza
Sta la tempesta ascosa:
remains the tempest hidden,

kosi riso talor gajoe pakato
Così riso talor gaio e pacato
so laughter, sometimes gay and peaceful

di kontento di dʒɔjaun lab:bro infjora
Di contento, di gioia un labbro infiora,
with contentment, with joy a lip touches,

mentre nel suo segreto il kɔr pjagato
Mentre nel suo segreto il cor piagato
while in[-the] its secret (depths) the heart wounded

saŋgɔʃ:ʃae si martɔra
S'angoscia e si martora.
[itself]-anguishes and itself tortures.

Come raggio di sol

See the sun's clear rays

Poet unknown
English version by
James P. Dunn

Antonio Caldara (ca. 1670-1736)
Editor unknown

Co - me rag - gio di sol   mi - te e se - re - no,
See   how the sun's clear   rays,   ra - diant and   lus - trous,

Co - me rag - gio di sol   mi - te e se - re   no
See   how the sun's clear   rays,   ra - diant and   lus -   trous,

Idiomatic translation: As a ray of sun, mild and serene,

rests upon the placid waves, while in the deep bosom of the sea the tempest remains hidden, so

laughter, sometimes gay and peaceful, with contentment and joy touches the lips,
while in its secret depths the wounded heart suffers anguish and martyrdom.

"Vergin, tutt'amor"

Solfeggio
solf<u>e</u>d:ʒo

Francesco Durante
frantʃesko dur<u>a</u>nte

Poetic idea

"Please hear my prayer for comfort in sadness!"

Background

As Italian singers became internationally famous, Italian singing teachers were also welcome visitors in every European country. Major composers wrote exercise pieces for their voice students. Such pieces are called *solfeggi*, a word derived from the syllables *sol* and *fa* in the musical scale. Solfeggi were sung either with syllable names or on pure vowels. This piece was originally composed for that purpose. More than a century later, words were added to this solfeggio, making it a prayer to the Virgin Mary. You may choose to sing this beautiful melody either with or without words.

Durante, esteemed as one of the most learned composers of his day, was the teacher of Pergolesi and many others. He was famous for his church music and his pedagogical works, but he wrote no operas.

Source

Solfèges d'Italie, no. 128 (Paris: Levèsque et Beche, 1st edition, 1772), copy in the Boston Public Library, Boston. Compiled by the publisher. For voice (soprano clef) and figured bass. Key: D minor. Meter: 12/4. Tempo: *Andante*. No text. (In later editions of the same book this piece is no. 150.)

The text, *"Vergin tutt'amor,"* first appeared anonymously in *Échos d'Italie*, edited by Lorenzo Pagans (Paris: Flaxland, before 1870), copy in the Sibley Music Library, Eastman School of Music, Rochester, NY. Same key, meter and tempo.

The familiar version was edited by Parisotti in *Arie Antiche*, Vol 1 (Milan: Ricordi, 1885). It has a typi-cally Romantic tempo marking, *Largo religioso*, and a pompous introduction. The familiar text, *"Vergin, tutto amor,"* is grammatically incorrect. As the phrase means "Virgin who is totally comprised of love," *"tutta"* refers to the Virgin Mary and requires a feminine ending. The phrase *"tutta amor"* can be correctly elided as *"tutt'amor"*.

v<u>e</u>rdzin t<u>u</u>t:tam<u>o</u>r
Vergin, tutt'amor,
Virgin,   all-love,

o m<u>a</u>dre di bont<u>a</u>de m<u>a</u>dre p<u>i</u>a
O madre di bontade, madre pia,
O mother of goodness, mother holy,

ask<u>o</u>lta d<u>o</u>ltʃe mar<u>i</u>a
Ascolta, dolce Maria,
hear,   sweet   Mary,

la v<u>o</u>tʃe del   pek:kat<u>o</u>r
La voce del   peccator.
the voice of-the sinner.

il   pj<u>a</u>nto s<u>u</u>o   ti   mw<u>o</u>va
Il   pianto suo   ti   muova,
[The] weeping his/her you let-move,

dzu<u>ŋ</u>gan a te i   sw<u>o</u>i lam<u>e</u>nti
Giungan a te i   suoi lamenti.
let-arrive to you [the] his/her laments.

suo   dw<u>o</u>l sw<u>o</u>i trist<u>j</u>at:ʃ<u>e</u>nti
Suo   duol, suoi   tristi accenti,
His/her sorrow, his/her sad   accents,

s<u>e</u>nti pjet<u>o</u>zo kwel tuo k<u>o</u>r.
Senti pietoso quel tuo cor.
let-hear merciful [that] your heart.

Vergin, tutt'amor/Solfeggio

Virgin, full of love

Lorenzo Pagans (?)
English version by
James P. Dunn

Francesco Durante (1684-1755)
Edited by John Glenn Paton

When this piece is sung with words, it is called *"Vergin, tutt'amor."* With-out words, it should be called *"Solfeggio."*
Idiomatic translation: Virgin, full of love, O mother of mercy, O holy mother, sweet Mary, hear

the voice of the sinner. Let a sinner's weeping move you, laments reach you.
Let a sinner's sorrow in sad accents be heard by your merciful heart.

"Danza, danza, fanciulla"

Solfeggio
solf<u>e</u>d:30

Francesco Durante
frant ʃesko dur<u>a</u>nte

Poetic idea

"Keep on dancing, because I love to see you!"

Background

Please read about *"Vergin, tutt'amor"* by the same composer. This song was also originally a solfeggio. If you sing it without words, the many repeated tones will be an interesting study in staccato singing.

Source

Solfèges d'Italie, no. 113 (Paris: Levèsque et Beche, 1st edition, 1772), copy in the Boston Public Library, Boston. Compiled by the publisher. For voice (soprano clef) and figured bass. Key: C minor. Meter: 6/4. Tempo: *Tempo giusto*. No text. (In later editions of the same book this piece is no. 137 and the tempo is *Allegro* or *Allegro moderato*.)

The text,*"Danza, danza, fanciulla,"* first appeared anonymously in *Échos d'Italie*, edited by Lorenzo Pagans (Paris: Flaxland, before 1870), copy in the Sibley Music Library, Eastman School of Music, Rochester, NY. Altered to B minor, 3/4, *Allegro con spirito*.

The familiar edition by Parisotti in *Arie Antiche*, Vol. 2 (Milan: Ricord, 1890), has an accompaniment in a late Romantic pianistic style and has several changes in the text.

d<u>a</u>ntsa fantʃ<u>u</u>l:la dʒent<u>i</u>le
Danza, fanciulla gentile,
Dance, girl gentle,

al m<u>i</u>o kant<u>a</u>r kant<u>a</u>re
Al mio cantar! (cantare,)
to[-the] my singing!

dʒ<u>i</u>ra led:ʒ<u>ɛ</u>ɾa sot:t<u>i</u>le
Gira, leggera, sottile,
Turn, light-one, slender-one,

al sw<u>ɔ</u>n del:l<u>ɔ</u>nde del mar
Al suon dell'onde del mar!
to[-the] sound of-the-waves of-the sea!

s<u>ɛ</u>ntil v<u>a</u>go rum<u>o</u>ɾe
Senti il vago rumore
Hear the lovely sound

del:l<u>a</u>uɾa skertso<u>z</u>a
Dell'aura scherzosa,
of-the-breeze playful,

ke p<u>a</u>rla in k<u>ɔ</u>ɾe
Che parla in core
which speaks in (your) heart

kon la<u>ŋ</u>gwido sw<u>ɔ</u>n
Con languido suon
with languid sound

e keinvit<u>a</u>l:la d<u>a</u>ntsa
E che invita alla danza
and which invites to-the dance

dap:pɾ<u>ɛ</u>s:so il m<u>a</u>ɾe mar
D'appresso il mare (mar)!
[of-]near the sea.

Danza, danza, fanciulla gentile / Solfeggio

Dance, o dance, gentle maiden

Lorenzo Pagans(?)
English version by
James P. Dunn

Francesco Durante (1684-1755)
Edited by John Glenn Paton

When this piece is sung with words, it is called *"Danza, danza, fanciulla."*
Without words, it should be called *"Solfeggio."*
*Idiomatic translation:*Dance, gentle girl, to my singing!

Turn, light and slender one, to the sound of the waves of the sea! Hear the
lovely sound of the playful breeze,

which speaks to the heart with a languid sound and which invites one to dance beside the sea!

Sento nel core

A page from a cantata manuscript owned by the G. Verdi Conservatory of Music, Milan, Italy. Above the music is written the phrase "Del [of] Signor Scarlatti." This copy is not the composer's autograph; it was made by a professional copyist. The original owner's name, found in the phrase "Per la [for] Signora Carlotta G?," has been crossed out. The later owner was Teresa de Cardenas. Notice that a sharp is used to raise B-flat to B.

"Quella fiamma"

Benedetto Marcello
benedet:to martʃɛl:lo

Poetic idea

"I shall never stop loving you and only you."

Background

Marcello, a prominent citizen of Venice, was considered an amateur composer, but an excellent one, respected by other prominent composers of his day. His greatest work was a musical setting of the first fifty Psalms in Italian verse for various combinations of voices and instruments.

Source

No early manuscript for this aria is known. It was published by Carl Banck in *Arien und Gesänge älterer Tonmeister* (Leipzig: Kistner, 1880). Key: G minor.

In Banck's collection, a source from which Parisotti borrowed eleven arias, *"Quella fiamma"* is preceded by a brief recitative, *"Il mio bel foco"*. The essential melodic line of the aria is consistent with Marcello's style, but Banck's piano interludes are in the bravura piano style of the late 1800s. This edition eliminates a four-measure vocal *coda* which is entirely foreign to Marcello's style and eliminates some of Banck's expression markings.

kwel:la fjam:ma ke mat:ʃɛnde
Quella fiamma che m'accende
That flame which me-kindles

pjatʃe tantoal:lalma mia
Piace tanto all'alma mia
pleases so-much to[-the]-soul mine

ke dʒam:mai sestingwera
Che giammai s'estinguerà.
that never itself-will-it-extinguish.

e seil fatoa voi mi rɛnde
E se il fato a voi mi rende,
And if [the] fate to you me returns,

vagi rai del mio bɛl sole
Vaghi rai del mio bel sole,
lovely rays of[-the] my beautiful sun,

altra lutʃeɛl:la non vwɔle
Altra luce ella non vuole
other light it (does) not want

ne voler dʒam:mai potra
Né voler giammai potrà.
nor to-wish ever will-it-be-able.

Quella fiamma

Flames within me

Poet unknown
English version by
James P. Dunn

Benedetto Marcello (1686-1739)
Edited by Carl Banck, 1880
Altered by John Glenn Paton

Idiomatic translation: That flame which sets me on fire pleases my soul so much

that it will never be extinguished.

And if fate returns me to you, lovely rays of the beautiful sun, my soul does not desire any other light, nor will it ever want any other.

"Nina"

Composer Unknown

Poetic idea

"My sweetheart is sick; someone please help me rouse her!" This song about a love-sick girl was sung as a serenade in the opera *The Three Silly Suitors*, but no one in the opera is named Nina and the song has no direct connection to the plot.

Background

"Nina" has been popular ever since it was introduced in London by an Italian opera company in 1749. The production featured music by various composers, most of them anonymous, and the book of "favorite songs" from the opera gave no composer's name for this song. From other sources the name of Giovanni Battista Pergolesi became attached to the song, but since he died in 1736 there is only the remotest chance that he had anything to do with it. Ciampi and Resta have been named as possible composers, but neither claim is backed up by documentary proof.

Source

The Favourite Songs in the Opera call'd Li tre cicisbei ridicoli (London: Walsh, 1749) copy in British Library, G811e(12). Original key: G minor. For voice (treble clef) and strings with figured bass. The first violin doubles the voice almost exactly throughout. All appoggiaturas are original, and are performed as sixteenth-notes. No ornaments have been added. For details of the history of *"Nina,"* see the article by Frank Walker in *Musical Times*, Dec. 1949.

The source of the familiar version is unknown. It has no introduction, and the melody begins with a two-note pick-up. The initial 7-measure phrase of the original is extended to a more conventional 8-measure phrase in the familiar version by means of an extra measure inserted after m10 (and m17). Ornamentation is included and not distinguished from the original notes.

tre   dʒorni son ke   nina
Tre   giorni son che Nina
Three   days   are that Nina

in lɛt:to se   ne   sta
In letto   se   ne   sta.
in bed   [herself from-there] stays.

il   son:no las:sas:sina
Il   sonno   l'assassina—
The slumber her-murders—

zveʎ:ʎatela, per pjeta
Svegliatela, per pietà!
waken-her,   for pity('s sake)!

e   tʃimbalie   timpanie   pif:feri
E   cimbali e   timpani e   pifferi,
And cymbals, and drums   and shawms,

zveʎ:ʎatemi   ninet:ta
Svegliatemi   Ninetta
waken-[for-]me little-Nina

perke at:ʃɔ   non dorma   pju
Perché (Acciò) non dorma   più.
so-that (so-that) not she-may-sleep more.

e   mentreil   sjor dot:tore
E   mentre il   sior dottore
And while   the sir doctor

a vizitarla va
A visitarla va,
to visit-her goes,

ninet:ta per amore
Ninetta   per amore
dear-Nina for love

in lɛt:to se   ne   sta
In letto   se   ne   sta.
in bed   [herself from-there] stays.

Nina

Poet unknown
English version by
James P. Dunn

Composer unknown
Edited by John Glenn Paton

Idiomatic translation:
(First stanza:) It has been three days that Nina has stayed in her bed.
(Second stanza:) And while the doctor is going to visit her,

(1.) Slumber is killing her. Waken her, please!

(2.) Nina is staying in bed on account of love.

(Both:) Cymbals, pipes, drums! Waken my little Nina,

net - ta,   sve - glia -   te - mi Ni - net - ta,   Per - ché non dor - ma
net - ta,   sve - glia -   te - mi Ni - net - ta,   Ac - ciò non dor - ma
net - ta,   pray,   wak -   en my Ni - net - ta,   And   let her sleep no

più_____   Per - ché non_ dor - ma   più.   Sve-glia-te - mi Ni - net - ta,   Ni -
più,_____   Ac - ciò non_ dor - ma   più.   Sve-glia-te - mi Ni - net - ta,   Ni -
more,_____   And_ let her_ sleep no   more.   Pray wak-en my Ni - net - ta,   Ni -

net - ta, Per - ché non_ dor - ma   più.
net - ta, Ac - ciò non_ dor - ma   più.
net - ta, And   let her_ sleep no_   more.

so that she won't sleep anymore.

"O del mio dolce ardor"

from *Paride ed Elena*
paride ed ɛlena

Christoph Willibald von Gluck
kristɔf vɪlːlibalt fɔn gluk

Poetic idea

"Beloved, I have not seen you yet, but you must be nearby!" The person who sings this is Paris, a prince of Troy, in the opera *Paris and Helen*.

According to the Greek legends told in Homer's *Iliad*, three goddesses asked Paris to judge which of them was most beautiful, and each offered him a bribe. Paris chose Aphrodite, the goddess of love, and his promised reward was the love of the most beautiful woman in the world, Helen, Queen of Sparta. As the opera begins, Paris arrives on a beach within sight of Sparta, and he joyfully anticipates seeing the woman of his dreams. (Later, Paris carried Helen away with him to Troy, and this caused the Trojan War.)

Background

Gluck was born in a village in what is now Bavaria (Germany), but Czech was his mother tongue. In Vienna, where opera audiences understood Italian, he composed his greatest successes, including *Orpheus and Euridice* and *Paris and Helen* (1770). He is remembered as a reformer because of the emotional directness and simplicity of his operas, in contrast to the artificiality and virtuosic vocal display of earlier operas.

Source

Paride ed Elena, full score of the opera, edited by Rudolf Gerber (Kassel: Barenreiter, 1954). For male soprano, oboe solo and strings. Original key: G minor. Meter: ₡.

Gluck wrote the appoggiaturas in m4 and m34; all other ornaments are editorial. Multiple cadenzas are offered; the singer may choose a comfortable one, invent a new one or sing none at all.

F. A. Gevaert included this aria in *Les Gloires de l'Italie* (Paris: Heugel, 1868), giving both the original vocal line and suggestions for vocal ornamentation on an additional staff. Gevaert worked from a score printed in Vienna in 1770, gave the meter as common time (₡), with the effect of slowing the tempo slightly.

The familiar edition, made by Parisotti in *Arie Antiche*, Vol. 2 (Milano: Ricordi, 1885), added more ornaments but did not print all of the original notes. Parisotti further slowed the tempo with a metronome marking of 46, which is inconsistent with the tempo indication of *Moderato*. The minor mode of the music (which symbolizes passion rather than sadness) and the incorrect metronome marking have misled most singers into performing this aria sadly and much too slowly.

o del mio doltʃeardor bramatodːʒɛtːto
O del mio dolce ardor bramato oggetto!
O of[-the] my sweet ardor desired object

laura ke tu respiri alfin respiro
L'aura che tu respiri alfin respiro.
the-air which you breathe at-last I-breathe.

ovuŋkweil gwardo io giro
Ovunque il guardo io giro
Wherever [the] (my) glance I turn

le tue vage sembjantse
Le tue vaghe sembianze
[the] your lovely features

amorein me dipindʒe
Amore in me dipinge,
Love [in] (for) me paints;

il mio pensjɛr si findʒe
Il mio pensier si finge
[the] my thought [to-itself] pretends (imagines)

le pju ljɛte sperantse
Le più liete speranze,
the most happy hopes

e nel dezio ke kosi mɛmpje il pɛtːto
E nel desio che così m'empie il petto
and in-the longing which thus [to-me-]fills [the] (my) bosom,

tʃɛrko te kjamo te, spɛro e sospiro
Cerco te, chiamo te, spero e sospiro!
I-seek you, I-call you, I-hope and I-sigh!

O del mio dolce ardor

O thou my own true love

Raniero de Calzabigi
English version by
James P. Dunn

Christoph Willibald von Gluck (1714-1787)
Vocal Ornamentation and Arrangement by
John Glenn Paton

Moderato, ♩ = 44 - 52

O   del mio dol - ce ar -
O   thou my own   true

dor_____   bra - ma - to og - get -
love,_____   O   thou, my   long -

to,   bra - ma - to og - get -   to,
ing,   de - sire   and long -   ing,

Idiomatic translation: O desired object of my sweet ardor,

L'au - re che tu re - spi - ri
Dear - est, at last I'm near_____ you,

al - fin re - spi - ro,
how I a - dore_____ you,

al - fin [Ah!_____] re -
Ah, love, [Ah!_____] a -

spi - ro.
dore_____ you!

O -
Wher -

the air which you breathe, at last I breathe.

15

vun - que il guar - do io gi - ro, Le tue
e'er my path - ways leads me, A fair

simile

17

va - ghe sem - bian - ze A - mo - re in me di - pin - ge: Il
vi - sion at - tends me, Ah, love, in dreams I hold you, In

19

mio pen - sier si fin - ge Le più lie -
ev - 'ry thought en - fold you, Hope and pas -

21 *f*

- - te spe - ran - -
- - *sion in - flames*

f

dim.

Wherever I turn my glances, love paints for me your lovely features. My
thoughts imagine the most happy hopes,

and in the longing which thus fills my bosom, I seek you, I call you, I
hope and I sigh.

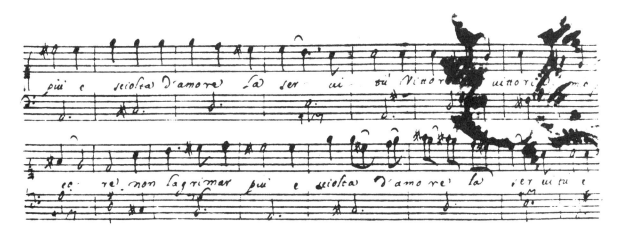

Vittoria, mio core

The front and reverse sides of page 200 from a cantata manuscript owned by the Civic Music Library, Bologna, Italy. The ink of the ornamented capital V has bled through to the reverse side of the paper. This is the work of a professional music copyist; it is not Carissimi's autograph.

"Caro mio ben"

Tommaso Giordani

tom:mazo dʒordani

Poetic idea

"Dear, I love you so much that when you stay away, I feel ill. Please be kind to me."

Background

English enthusiasm for Italian opera continued throughout the 1700s, and it continues today. Sixty years after Bononcini composed *Griselda* for London, Tommaso Giordani composed *"Caro mio ben"* for a concert there. A native of Naples, Giordani lived most of his life in London and published many vocal and instrumental compositions there.

Source

"The Favorite Song as Sung by Sigr. Tenducci at the Pantheon & Mr. Abel's Concerts, Composed by Sigr. Giordani" (London: Preston, 1782?), copy at University of Kansas at Lawrence. For voice (treble clef) and 4-part strings. Key: F.

The accompaniment in this edition is a reduction of the scoring for strings. The staccato markings given here are present in the string parts; one must judge whether they sound well when played on a piano.

The double grace-notes in the accompaniment and those in the voice in m29 and m30 are included in the original publication. The remaining ornaments are adapted from a manuscript volume of miscellaneous music that belonged to an unnamed British lady in 1788 or later: Additional 54,331, British Library, London. The ornaments have no particular authority, but they certainly reflect the amount and kind of ornamentation that a cultivated listener expected to hear.

Bibliography

John Glenn Paton, *"Caro mio ben*: Some Early Sources," *NATS Bulletin*, Nov/Dec. 1981.

The familiar edition, edited by Parisotti in 1890, names the composer as Giuseppe Giordani (no relation to Tommaso). The evidence for Tommaso as the actual composer is given in the above article.

karo mi̯o bɛn
Caro mio ben,
Dear, my   beloved,

kredimialmen
Credimi   almen,
believe-me at-least,

sɛntsa di te
Senza di te
without   [of] you

laŋgwiʃ:ʃeil   kɔr
languisce il   cor.
languishes [the] (my) heart.

il   tu̯o fedel
Il   tuo   fedel
[The] your faithful-one

sospi̯raoŋ:ŋor
Sospira ognor.
sighs   always.

tʃɛs:sa krudel
Cessa, crudel,
Cease,   cruel-one,

tanto   rigor
Tanto   rigor!
so-much severity.

Caro mio ben

Ah, dearest love

Poet unknown
English version by
James P. Dunn

Tommaso Giordani (1730-1806)
Edited by John Glenn Paton

Larghetto, ♩ = 36 - 42

dolce

Ca - ro mio bɛn,
Ah,   dear - est   love,

Cre - di - mi al - men,
If   you should leave,

Sɛn - za di   te
Heav - en a - bove

Lan - gui - sce il
knows how I'd

Idiomatic translation: My dear beloved, believe me at least, without you

my heart languishes. Your faithful one always sighs; cruel one, cease so much punishment.

"Nel cor più non mi sento"

from *L'amor contrastato*
lam<u>o</u>r kontrast<u>a</u>to

Giovanni Paisiello
dʒov<u>a</u>n:ni paizj<u>ɛ</u>l:lo

Poetic idea

"Why don't I feel as well as usual? Love is driving me crazy!" The person who sings this is Rachelina, "a rich mill-owner and imprudent in love," according to the libretto. She is being pursued by three lovers, so it is no wonder that she is confused.

The scene of the opera is Rachelina's rustic home in the countryside near Naples. When the curtain rises, Rachelina is working, something that women in earlier operas seldom did.

Background

Paisiello was the most popular comic composer of his time. While he served at the court of Catherine the Great of Russia, he composed *The Barber of Seville*, which was beloved for over 30 years, until it was replaced by Rossini's *Barber of Seville*. Paisiello's graceful melodies influenced many other composers, even Mozart.

"Nel cor più non mi sento" comes from *L'Amor contrastato* (The Hard-Won Love), produced in Naples in 1789, and performed throughout Europe for many years. In other cities the opera was sometimes titled *La molinara* or *La bella molinara (The Beautiful Miller-Woman)*. This aria became enormously popular; famous stars sang elaborate ornamentations, and Beethoven wrote piano variations on it.

Audiences remembered *"Nel cor..."* not only because it is simple, but also because they heard it several times in the scene. It is sung by Rachelina, then by a tenor suitor, Colloandro, and the ending is repeated as a duet. After a recitative it is sung by a baritone suitor, Pistofolo, with the ending again repeated as a duet.

Source

L'amor contrastato, autograph score of the opera, in the library of the Conservatorio di Musica, San Pietro a Majella, Naples, Rari 3.1.3.4; this would be the most authoritative source, but most of the aria is missing from it. Manuscripts in other libraries have been consulted, but because of the lack of a complete primary source, this edition conforms to the published score of the opera: *La Molinara ossia L'amor contrastato*, edited by A. Rocchi (Florence: Maggio Musicale, 1962).

The familiar version, made by Parisotti in *Arie Antiche*, Vol. 1 (Milan: Ricordi, 1855), consists of m1–m28 only. The ornaments given are acceptable in style, but not unique nor authoritative. The singer should feel free to explore many possible ornaments.

---

nel kɔr pju non mi s<u>e</u>nto
Nel cor più non mi sento
In-the heart more not myself I-feel

bril:l<u>a</u>r la dʒoventu
Brillar la gioventù.
sparkle [the] youth.

kadʒ<u>o</u>n del mio torm<u>e</u>nto
Cagion del mio tormento,
Cause of[-the] my torment,

amor tʃ<u>ai</u> k<u>o</u>lpa tu
Amor, ci hai colpa tu.
Love, there have guilt you.

mi st<u>u</u>t:siki mi m<u>a</u>stiki
Mi stuzzichi, mi mastichi,
Me you-excite, me you-bite,

mi p<u>u</u>ndʒiki mi p<u>i</u>t:siki
Mi pungichi, mi pizzichi;
me you-prick, me you-pinch;

ke k<u>o</u>saɛ kw<u>e</u>staɔim<u>e</u>
Che cosa è questa, ohimè?
What thing is this, alas?

pjet<u>a</u>
Pietà, pietà, pietà!
Pity!

am<u>o</u>rɛun tʃ<u>ɛ</u>rto ke
Amor è un certo che,
Love is a certain something

ke delir<u>a</u>r mi fa
Che delirar mi fa!
which be-delirious me makes!

Nel cor più non mi sento

My heart ne'er leaps with gladness

Giuseppe Palomba
English version by
James P. Dunn

Giovanni Paisiello (1740-1816)
Edited by John Glenn Paton

(Text for a female singer:) Nel cor più non mi sen - to, Bril-
(Text for a male singer:) Ti sen - to, sì, ti sen - to, Bɛl
My heart ne'er leaps with glad - ness, Youth's

(Examples of ornamentation)

In the opera, a woman sings the first stanza and a man sings the second, then both singers sing the conclusion, m30-m45. The alternate vocal line provides examples of appropriate ornaments which the singer may use in singing the melody (the two lines are not to be sung simultaneously!). The aria may also be performed as a solo, ending at m28.

Idiomatic translation:
(Female:) No longer do I feel youth sparkle in my heart.
(Male:) I hear you, yes, I hear you, lovely flower of youth.

lar la gio - ven - tù; Ca - gion del mio tor - men - to A -
fior di gio - ven - tù; Ca - gion del mio tor - men - to,
glow it feels no more, All full of woe and sad - ness, 'Tis

mor, ci hai col - pa tu.) Mi stuz - zi - chi, mi mas - ti - chi, Mi
A - ni - ma mia, sei tu.) It nips at me, it nudg - es me, It
love the fault must bear.

pun - gi - chi, mi piz - zi - chi, Che co - sa è ques - ta, oi - mè? Pie -
nee - dles me, it pinch - es me, Ah me, what can I do? Ah,

(F.) The cause of my torment? Love, you are the guilty one. You excite me, bite me, prick me, pinch me; what is this, alas?

(M.) The cause of my torment? My soul, it is you! you excite me, bite me, prick me, pinch me; what is this, alas?

tà, pie - tà, pie - tà,_____ A - mo - reɛun cɛr - to
tà, pie - tà, pie - tà,_____ Quel vi - so ha un cɛr - to
love, have care, have care,_____ 'Tis you in - deed, I

che, Che de - li - rar mi fa!
che, Che de - li - rar mi fa!
know, That cause all my de - spair!

(ah,_____)

1.

2.

Mi stuz - zi - chi, Mi pun - gi - chi,

fa! mi mas - ti-chi, mi

(F.) Pity, pity! Love is a certain something that drives me crazy!
(M.) Pity, pity! That face has a certain something that drives me crazy!

CAU. ALESSANDRO SCARLATTI MRO DI CAPPEL·NAPOLITANO

Alessandro Scarlatti

This portrait hangs in the Civic Music Library, Bologna, Italy. Scarlatti is identified with the title of *Cavaliere* and wears a jeweled official decoration. He is also identified as "*Maestro di Cappella Napolitano,*" or Neapolitan conductor, his title at the court. On the desk behind him is an ink pot with quill pens and a copy of one of his finest cantatas, "*Alfin m'ucciderete.*"

"Se i miei sospiri"

François Joseph Fétis
frãswa ʒɔzɛf fetis

Poetic idea

"I would bear suffering, even death, if I could only please that person!"

Background

This song was first sung by a tenor in Paris in 1833 at a concert devoted to music from the 1600s. The concert described the song as a "church aria...composed by Stradella (1667) ...a masterpiece of religious expression and tender sentiment." Fétis, the organizer of the concert, claimed to own Stradella's original manuscript, but he did not show it to anyone.

"Se i miei sospiri" was published in Paris in 1838 with string accompaniment in D minor. In 1843 Fétis published the song in C minor with a piano accompaniment and new words, *"Pietà, Signore"*. The new version was soon re-printed in Italy and other countries, and became famous. It was also published with still other texts, including *"Ave verum corpus"*.

In 1866 a French musicologist, P. Richard, found the text of *"Se i miei sospiri"* set to different music in an oratorio by Alessandro Scarlatti, *The Martyrdom of St. Theodosia* (1693). In the oratorio these words are sung by a man who is in love with Theodosia; his frustrated passion becomes the cause of her death. Richard noted with some irony that the "tender sentiment" of the text is not at all religious and also that Fétis had not made his sources available to the public.

After Fétis died, his extensive musical library was bought by the Royal Library in Brussels; there was no Stradella aria. By that time many persons recognized that the musical style of the aria was inconsistent with Stradella's time and that Stradella could not be the true composer. Without all of the above facts, some writers suggested various musicians who might have enjoyed tricking the public with a forgery. Some mentioned Rossini, but without evidence. A recent music encyclopedia states that *"Pietà, Signore"* appears in an opera called *Stradella* by Niedermeyer, but that is not true. All available evidence points to Fétis as the true composer.

Source

(1) text and vocal part, *"Se i miei sospiri"* in *Kirchen-Arien* (Leipzig: Peters, 19??). (*"M'alletta"* has been corrected to *"m'allettò".*) (2) accompaniment, *"Pietà, Signore"* in *Recueil des Morceaux de Musique Ancienne*, vol. 3 (Paris: Société de Musique Religieuse et Classique, 1843). For voice (tenor clef) and piano. Key: C minor.

Bibliography

(1) P. Richard, *"Stradella et les Contarini,"* Le Menestrel, March 11, 1866. (2) Guido Salvetti, *"Le verità di una falsificazione,"* Chigiana, vol. 19 (Florence: Olschki, 1988). These articles, brought to my attention by Prof. Eleanor McCrickard of the University of North Carolina, assemble all of the above evidence.

sei   mjɛi sospiɾi
Se i   miei sospiri,
If [the] my   sighs,

ɔ   dio plakas:seɾo
Oh Dio! placassero
Oh God! would-placate

lɛmpjo   sembjante
L'empio   sembiante
the-impious countenance

ke mal:let:tɔ
Che m'allettò:
that me-enticed,

tut:ti   martiɾi
Tutti i   martiri
all   the sufferings

ke   mɔrte das:seɾo
Che morte dassero,
that death would-give,

sɛmpre kostante
Sempre costante
always   constant,

io sof:friɾɔ
Io soffrirò.
I will-suffer.

Se i miei sospiri

Hear me, O heavens

Poet unknown
English version by
James P. Dunn

François Joseph Fétis (1784-1871)

Idiomatic translation: If my sighing, O God! would placate that inhuman countenance

that enticed me, all the suffering that death would give, always constant, I will suffer.

sof - fri - rò.
cruel - est blows.

Se i miei so - spi - ri, Se i miei so - spi -
Could sighs of long - ing, Could all these ar -

- ri, oh Dio!__ pla - cas - se - ro L'em - pio sem - bian - te,
- dent sighs__ of__ yearn - ing Soothe those harsh glanc - es,

L'em - pio sem - bian - te Che m'al - let - tò,
Proud, haugh - ty glanc - es That__ so en - thrall me,

A Baroque Opera House

Gold leaf covers almost every decorative detail in this exceptionally rich opera theater in Bayreuth, Germany. It was designed in 1748 by two members of the Bibiena family, who for four generations were the leading Italian architects of theaters and designers of scenery.

This view is from the stage, which is still occasionally used for concerts. The railing at the bottom of the picture separates the orchestra and the audience. The theater's level floor could be filled with armchairs for opera performances or used as a dance floor on festive occasions. The Margrave of Bayreuth sat in the central box on the first tier of boxes. Most of the audience sat in the three levels of boxes that form a horseshoe shape. Persons who sat in the side boxes had a limited view of the stage, but excellent opportunities to view each other.

"Se tu m'ami"

Alessandro Parisotti
ales:sandro parizɔt:ti

Poetic idea

"Yes, I love you, but I love other men, too!"

Background

This song was first made public in 1885 in an anthology. It was presented as a work of Giovanni Battista Pergolesi (1710–1736), but no scholar today accepts it as genuine. Since no early manuscript of *"Se tu m'ami"* has ever been found, and the other songs in the book come from known sources, it is now believed that Parisotti wrote it himself. Parisotti was an able musician who sincerely loved early music, but he was not above publishing other editors' work as if it were his own (international copyrights were not yet enforced).

To make his forgery seem more genuine, Parisotti used a poem from the 1700s. The Italian poet Rolli lived in London and wrote opera libretti for both Handel and Bononcini.

Sources

Text, Paolo Rolli, *Di canzonette e di cantate libri due* (London: T. Edlin, 1727); music, Alessandro Parisotti, *Arie Antiche*, Vol. 1 (Milan: Ricordi, 1885). Key: F minor.

Rolli's poem is printed above with the original spelling and punctuation; in the music the text is modernized. Parisotti changed "Silvio" to "Silvia," as if the singer herself were picking a rose; this is incorrect. What the text says is that a typical man would reject a former lover in favor of a new one. The singer says that she would not follow this example, because she is able to love more than one man at a time.

The style of performance should be late Romantic; Baroque ornamentation and Classical strictness of tempo would both be inappropriate here.

se tu mami   se sospiri
Se tu m'ami, se sospiri
If you me-love, if you-sigh

sol per me dʒentil pastor
Sol per me, gentil Pastor;
only for me, kind   shepherd,

ɔ   dolor de   twɔi martiri
O   dolor de   tuoi martiri,
I-have sorrow [of-the] (for) your sufferings,

ɔ   dilɛt:to del   tuamor
O   diletto del   tu' amor:
I-have pleasure [of-the] (in) your love,

ma se pɛnsi   ke solɛt:to
Ma se pensi   che soletto
but if you-think that alone

io ti dɛb:ba riamar
Io ti debba riamar,
I you must   love-in-return,

pastorɛl:lo sɛi   sod:ʒɛt:to
Pastorello, sei   soggetto
little-shepherd, you-are subject

fatʃilmɛntea tiŋgan:nar
Facilmente a t'ingannar.
easily   to yourself-deceive.

bɛl:la rɔza porporina
Bella Rosa porporina
Beautiful rose red

ɔd:ʒi silvjo ʃeʎ:ʎera
Oggi Silvio sceglierà,
today silvio will-choose;

kon la skuza del:la spina
Con la scusa della Spina
with the excuse of-the thorn

doman pɔi la spret:sera
Doman poi la sprezzerà.
tomorrow then it he-will-despise.

ma deʎ:ʎwɔminil konsiʎ:ʎo
Ma degli Uomini'l consiglio
But of[-the] men   the advice

io per me   non segwirɔ
Io per me   non seguirò,
I for myself not   will-follow:

non perke mi   pjatʃeil dʒiʎ:ʎo
Non perché mi   piace il Giglio
not because to-me pleases the lily

ʎaltri fjɔri spret:serɔ
Gli altri Fiori sprezzerò.
the other flowers will-I-despise.

Se tu m'ami

If you love me

Paolo Antonio Rolli
English version by
James P. Dunn

Alessandro Parisotti (1853-1913)

Idiomatic translation: If you love me, if you sigh only for me, kind shepherd,

I feel sorrow for your suffering; I feel pleased that you love me. But if you think that I must love only you, little shepherd, you are easily subject to self-deception.

Today Silvio chooses a beautiful red rose, but with the excuse that the
thorns prick, he will despise it tomorrow. The advice of men, I myself won't follow.
Just because the lily pleases me, I won't despise the other flowers.

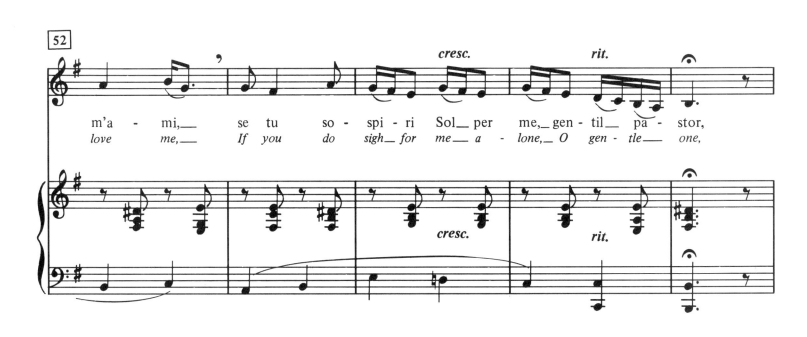

The Sounds of Italian

Italian is the favored language of great singers not only because of the beautiful music composed in that language, but also because the sounds of Italian are favorable to good singing. In learning to sing Italian correctly, one learns vocal habits that improve the singing of other languages as well.

These are some points of contrast between English and Italian:

- *English emphasizes consonants, Italian emphasizes vowels.* Strong emotions are conveyed in English by strong consonants, but in Italian by resonant vowels. Most English syllables end in consonants, but most Italian syllables end with vowel sounds.

- *English speech is often broken by pauses, Italian almost never.* English speakers often stop their tone in order to emphasize the coming word or to keep two vowels from running together, but Italians speak with continuous legato.

- *English vowels may change color, Italian vowels are constant.* The vowels in English "low" and "lay" are diphthongs, which change quality while they are being said; the similar Italian vowels in "lo" and "le" do not change quality no matter how long they last.

- *English consonants sometimes change the color of nearby vowels, Italian ones do not.* When an English vowel is followed by "l" or "r" (as in "steel" and "steer"), the consonant is likely to affect the vowel; in Italian this is not allowed to happen and the vowel remains pure.

- *Some consonants are pronounced toward the back of the mouth in English, but toward the front of the mouth in Italian.* In American speech, "r" involves the back of the tongue, but in Italian "r" is flipped or rolled with the tongue-tip.

- *Italian consonants in general are weaker than English consonants.* The sounds [p], [t] and [k] are sung without any escaping puff of air, and other consonant sounds are also weaker.

This last statement has a great exception: Italian double consonants are strong and clear. Compared with single consonants, double consonants take much more time to pronounce, even if they interrupt the musical line. For instance, in *petto* [pɛt:to], the symbol [:] means "hold the consonant position." The first [t] stops the tone, and there is a brief silence before the second [t] begins it again.

Diphthongs

When two or more vowels are sung on a quick note, the note may be divided evenly among the vowels. When the note is longer, one vowel is selected to be the "syllabic vowel." It fills most of the note value, and the other vowels are pronounced quickly at the beginning or end of the note. This is especially important for the possessive pronouns *mio, tuo, suo,* and their various forms; in this book the syllabic vowels of these words are underlined for emphasis.

An Italian poet regards consecutive vowels and semi-vowels as belonging to one syllable, even if they belong to different words. For instance, in the phrase *degli uomini* the sounds [iwɔ] belong to one syllable and they are sung on only one note. In this book such combinations are indicated by a curved line connecting the words and the syllabic vowel is underlined (see m39 of *"Se tu m'ami"*, page 149).